R.B.
A Prophet
in the Land

Rienk Bouke Kuiper 1886-1966

Edward Heerema

R.B.
A Prophet in the Land

Rienk Bouke Kuiper
Preacher – Theologian – Churchman

*"And he will know that there is
a prophet in Israel" (II Kings 5:8).*

PAIDEIA PRESS LTD.
Jordan Station, Ontario, Canada

Canadian Cataloguing in Publication Data

Heerema, Edward
  R.B., a prophet in the land

ISBN 0-88815-054-7

1. Kuiper, Rienk Bouke, 1886-1966.   2. Reformed
Church in America – Clergy – Biography.
3. Clergy – United States – Biography.   I. Title.

BX9543.K84H43   1986   285.7'32'0924   C86-094943-5

Back cover: R.B. brings up the rear descending muleback into the Grand Canyon in 1923.

Cover design by Rachelle Longtin

ISBN 0-88815-054-7
Printed in Canada

Contents

To the memory of Marietta —
so much like her father in many ways

Preface

I was enthralled. Never before had I heard preaching like that. His pulpit presence demanded one's attention. His language was current and fresh, the biblical message came through convincingly, his illustrations were gripping, his personal appeal powerful. The preacher was R.B. Kuiper and I was hearing him for the first time. He was president of Calvin College and was guest preacher in his former church, the Sherman Street Christian Reformed Church. I had just recently enrolled at the college.

My impression of him on that occasion has always stayed with me. The remarkable person I heard that Sunday night in that packed church has always remained a remarkable person for me, also when I came to know him intimately as my father-in-law. A striking fact of his career bolsters that enduring opinion of the man. He in his time became head of three noted Calvinistic institutions, namely, Calvin College, Westminster Theological Seminary and Calvin Theological Seminary. That outstanding record will probably never be repeated. He filled all of these responsible positions with distinction, even though his service at Calvin Seminary was under difficult circumstances.

Many people who have heard R.B. preach have said that he was the best preacher they ever heard. Not a few said that in their judgment he was the best preacher the Christian Reformed Church has produced. I am disposed to agree with that assessment. These factors have placed me under strong compulsion to write this book, especially since his personal papers came into my possession by way of inheritance. My hope and prayer is that God may be pleased to use this effort of mine to the praise of His glory and to a warm realization on the part of many that in R.B. Kuiper the Lord had a prophet in the land.

What about that name Rienk Bouke? It is unusual, to be sure. The story is that he was named after an uncle and an aunt who were rather well-to-do and their namesake might be expected to benefit from that fact some day. It never happened, and he was stuck with that name. So he got to be known generally as R.B. Once a letter addressed to Rev. Rienk Bouke Kuiper was posted on the bulletin board at Westminster Seminary. A student wrote these words next to the name on the envelope, "I wouldn't use em either."

One important facet of his rich career of service to Christ's Kingdom is passed by in this book, regrettably so. It has to do with the role he played in the ardent support and advocacy of Christian education in the day school at every level—elementary school, high school, college, university. His speeches and writings for this cause could easily fill a good-sized book. He was a member of a board that sought to establish a Christian University. Unfortunately the project never got off the ground. The failure to include a chapter on this facet of his career is not an oversight. With so much material available to me I felt that I should concentrate on those three areas of his labors where he was primarily involved, namely, as preacher, theologian and churchman.

The following chapters will reveal that R.B. was involved in many a controversy. I have pretty much allowed him to be the judge in determining what should be included in this book so far as controversial material is concerned. If he felt an issue was important enough for him to enter the arena of debate over it, I have not wanted to second-guess him in the matter. For a number of personal reasons it would have been comfortable to leave out some of the controversial material these chapters contain. But I had to try to present an authentic portrait of R.B. Kuiper. His zeal for the integrity of the truth of the Word of God is essential to that portrait.

It is now about twenty years since R.B. left this earthly scene. That is a considerable span of time in this fast-paced age. There was a sparkle of contemporaneity about him that continues to shine. He still speaks to our time because he rarely dealt with the trivialities of the moment when he preached or wrote. He sought to articulate that which God spoke in His timely and timeless Word. Not infrequently citations from R.B.'s writings appear in current religious books and periodicals.

Because of my close personal association with R.B. Kuiper there may be some who think that I was privileged to acquire a lot of inside information that R.B. was privy to in his sensitive positions. Nothing could be farther from the truth. He was most discreet in what he told me. Often I learned of some development from other sources and he would be surprised when I asked him about it. Even then he might still be very close-mouthed. He was not a man to betray a trust.

My close association with R.B. gave me a little problem as to my choice of personal pronouns in speaking of him. At times I have felt free to use pronouns in the first person. Rigidly uniform usage of third person pronouns would, it seemed to me, come across to the reader as being rather stilted.

Many people have been most helpful to me in the preparation of this book. To all of them I am very grateful. I retreat before the thought of compiling a complete list of these helpful people, and I would not like to omit any. So I shall single out three people for special mention. First of all there is my brother-in-law Dr. Klaudius Kuiper. Without his input of innumerable details of the Kuiper family life the writing of this book would have been next to impossible. Almost of equal value has been the help of Sarah Venema. When she was still a girl named Sarah Flanders she became acquainted with the Kuiper family when R.B. was pastor of the Sherman Street Christian Reformed Church. She looked after the Kuiper children and ever since has been almost a member of the family. Then there is my wife Bertha. Her help in typing and proofreading contributed much. Her tending to a host of details in day-to-day living allowed me to stay at my desk for the countless hours that this project required. And she never uttered even a sigh of complaint.

I also want to express my appreciation for useful information given me by the Alumni Association of Morgan Park Academy and by the keepers of the archives at the Library of Calvin College and Seminary, the Westminster Seminary Library and the Grand Rapids Public Library. The personnel at the Calvin College and Seminary Archives were especially generous with their assistance. The office of Secretary of the

Seminary at Princeton Theological Seminary was also helpful.

Finally, I wish to register my thanks for the valuable comments and suggestions made by a number of people who graciously took the time to read the manuscript. Of these I mention first of all my daughter, Professor Mary Dykstra of Dalhousie University in Halifax. Others to whom I am indebted are Dr. Edmund P. Clowney, President Emeritus of Westminster Theological Seminary; Dr. Peter Y. De Jong of Mid-America Reformed Seminary; Dr. Fred H. Klooster of Calvin Theological Seminary; and Murray Forst Thompson, Esq., who as a close associate of J. Gresham Machen was active for many years in the affairs of Westminster Seminary and the Orthodox Presbyterian Church.

I conclude this preface on a sentimental note. All the while that I was writing this book I was sitting in the old wooden swivel chair that R.B. sat in as he labored in his study all the years that I knew him. Perhaps this fact will lend a measure of authenticity to the story that unfolds in the ensuing chapters.

Cape Coral, Florida   Edward Heerema

Chapter 1

The First Five Years

With that special sparkle in his eye R.B. Kuiper said that he had studied abroad. Those who were well acquainted with his life story knew that he had not spent time overseas as a student. The sparkle remained in his eye as he met the questioning looks of his friends by saying that he spent the first five years of his life in Europe, and he learned more in those five years than in any subsequent period of his life.

Like his shining eyes, his words glistened with the humor and the down to earth good sense that were so characteristic of the man. Well, what did he learn in those first five years?

There is no point in dwelling on those countless things that any child learns in the first years of his life. Rather we shall take a good look at certain influences marking those formative years that had so much to do with the making of the remarkable man that many people came to know as R.B. Kuiper or simply as R.B.

Rienk Bouke Kuiper was born January 31, 1886 in the village of Garrelsweer, province of Groningen in the far northern part of The Netherlands. The future minister was the sixth child born to Rev. and Mrs. Klaas Kuiper, who occupied the manse of a Reformed church at a time when stirring events were happening in the churches of The Netherlands. These events form a strikingly fitting backdrop for the life that began on January 31, 1886. More about that later.

Two more children were born to Dominee and Mevrouw Klaas Kuiper. So by the time Rienk was five years old he was one of a lively family of eight children—six sons and two daughters. Growing up with so much life around him, Rienk simply could

11

not develop into a reclusive type of person. The uproariously good times the Kuiper siblings would have when they got together in their later years had their beginning in the busy manse at Garrelsweer.

The Parents

Young Rienk early learned to respect authority in the person of his father. He was a loving father who was also a stern disciplinarian. The children were all gifted with a good mind and fertile imagination. The mischief the six boys might conceive was restrained by the inescapable piercing eyes of the father. Those sharp eyes still look down on you searchingly from the wall of the council room of the Garrelsweer church, where Dominee Kuiper's picture hangs third in the gallery of former pastors.

The deep regard that the children developed for their father was enhanced by the prestige Dominee Kuiper enjoyed as a pastor. A minister of the gospel, like a physician or lawyer, was a special person in Holland. The man called "Dominee" was looked upon with a respect bordering on reverence. His social position was considerably above that of the average person occupying the pews. Added to that was the physical location of the preacher as he proclaimed the Word of God. His pulpit was about ten feet above the floor of the church auditorium. It is not at all uncommon for children to think of the preacher as God. What went through a little boy's mind as he listened to his father hold forth from his lofty perch?

Alongside the strict father was the mother, whose maiden name was Maaike de Bruyn. Although details regarding her character are scarce, one fact stands out: she had an infectious sense of humor. Her laughter filled the home with a lightheartedness that softened the sternness of the father. Mother Kuiper often could not restrain her sense of fun at the mischievous antics of her sons. One acquaintance spoke of her as a "cut-up." Sometimes as the boys grew up the church bench would shake as she struggled to suppress her laughter at some sly prank perpetrated by one of the lads sitting piously in a row next to her. On more than one occasion the father came down from the pulpit to restore order in the family pew, with a surprised and amused congregation looking on.

Behind the church at Garrelsweer was something that any boy would find wonderful—a canal. Fortunately for Mother Kuiper the canal was not so close to the house. The manse was on the other side of the church. But fear of having one of her children fall into the canal was a constant worry for the lady of the manse. Little Rienk had no such concerns. From his older siblings—firstborn Barend, for instance, was about eight years older—he learned that one could go to distant and wonderful places on the canal, to the big city of Groningen twelve miles to the south, or to the port of Delfzijl to the east. So a life that would go far began to expand as Rienk played and had dreamy glimpses of faraway places on the banks of Damster diep, that fascinating waterway behind the church.

Father, mother, siblings, the manse, the father's pulpit, the canal—all had their part in the making of R.B. Kuiper. Equally important was the spiritual and intellectual milieu into which he was born. Events and forces converging at that point in history did much to shape the mold from which would come a mind that would be as clearly focused and strong as it was scintillating.

The Secession Background

Early in Klaas Kuiper's pastorate at Garrelsweer an event took place that helps us to understand the ideological climate that prevailed when and where his sixth child was born. That event was the fiftieth anniversary of the establishment of the congregation. The church was born on October 24, 1835. That date, let it be carefully noted, comes very close to a momentous happening in the history of the Reformed churches in Holland. We refer to the *Afscheiding* (Secession), which took place in 1834. In response to disciplinary actions taken against their pastor Hendrik De Cock, the congregation at Ulrum seceded from the established church on October 13-14, 1834. This was the beginning of a large exodus from the state church. At bottom the movement was prompted by keen dissatisfaction among the plain people with decay in confessional loyalty and in ecclesiastical procedures in the state church. Reaction against those ever-emerging twin evils of liberalism and ecclesiastical bureaucratic autocracy sparked the Secession of 1834. Mention must be made of a religious revival stemming from the *Reveil* (Awakening), which was a renewal of religion among people of learning and social standing. In this movement the writings of the poets Willem Bilderdijk and Isaac Da Costa were most effective, and widely read.

A check of the map of The Netherlands reveals something most interesting at this point. Ulrum, where the Secession had its start, is located about eighteen miles due west of Garrelsweer. In other words, this area of northern Holland is the place where this rebellion flourished against the established church, its liberalism and autocracy. The movement spread rapidly throughout Holland, but it was strongest in the northern provinces of Groningen, Friesland, Drenthe and Overijssel. The newly formed denomination, named Christian Reformed Church, established its own theological seminary at Kampen in the province of Overijssel in the year 1854.

The church at Garrelsweer, established so soon after the Secession of 1834, was formed and nourished by deep loyalty to God's Word and great strength of character. The Seceders (*Afgescheidenen*)[1] suffered persecution, economic and otherwise. Rev. K. Kuiper was reared in a small seceder church in the province of Drenthe. His parents operated a small farm. He attended the theological school at Kampen. His first pastorate was at Oud Loosdrecht, province of Utrecht, where persecution had been especially severe at the time of the Secession. Oud Loosdrecht, Ferwerd in Friesland and Garrelsweer—all three of the congregations that Klaas Kuiper served in Holland were of the same kind. That was the strong stuff on which the family of Klaas Kuiper was nurtured.

Abraham Kuyper

The burning convictions which fired the Secession of 1834 were not spent at the time of the fiftieth anniversary of the Garrelsweer church. On the contrary, these convictions were strengthened and sharpened because of the work of a man of genius whose influence was mounting rapidly during the time of

Rev. K. Kuiper's career as a pastor in The Netherlands. That man of genius was Abraham Kuyper, who had served large churches in the cities of Utrecht and Amsterdam. His writings were voluminous and rang with the principles of Augustine and Calvin, set forth in fresh language and new perspectives on Christianity as it relates to all of life. Two earlier writings reveal the man's bent of mind. These influential books were entitled *Uniformity, The Curse of Modern Life* (1869) and *Modernism, A Deceptive Mirage on Christian Territory* (1871).[2] Early in his career as pastor he had turned from his university-bred liberalism to a genuinely biblical and Calvinistic mindset. Under the Holy Spirit this remarkable conversion happened largely because of the impact of conversations the youthful minister had with members of his first church in the village of Beesd, province of Utrecht. These humble believers, especially the godly woman Pietje Baltus, had things to say to their young pastor with his liberal ideas.

This highly gifted man's achievements were nothing short of prodigious. He edited two significant publications, a daily newspaper called *De Standaard* and also a weekly organ named *De Heraut* (The Herald). He organized a Christian political party and became a member of parliament. He was chosen prime minister of Holland in 1901, serving in the capacity until 1905. No less impressive was the founding of the Free University of Amsterdam in 1880—"Free" because it was not under state control, an arrangement quite in keeping with Kuyper's insistence upon the principle that there are different spheres of sovereignty in life which must exercise their own God-given authority and function.

All Holland was stirred by the extraordinary performance of Abraham Kuyper. What caused the greatest stir occurred in the very year Rienk Bouke Kuiper was born—1886. In that year Abraham Kuyper led a second large Secession out of the Netherlands state church. The new group was called the Reformed Free Church. Largely due to the leadership of Kuyper a union was brought about in 1892 between the Seceders of 1834 and those of 1886. The new church was named Reformed Churches in The Netherlands (*Gereformeerde Kerken in Nederland*).[3]

Any description of the milieu into which R.B. Kuiper was born would be incomplete without reference to another Chris-

tian thinker whose work made a marked impression on the life
of Klaas Kuiper and his family. That thinker was Herman
Bavinck, who became professor at the theological school at
Kampen six years after Klaas Kuiper began his ministry. Bavinck
later took a position as professor at the Free University of
Amsterdam, thus becoming a colaborer with Abraham Kuyper.
Bavinck too was a thoroughly biblical scholar whose work was
characterized by depth and breadth. His work together with that
of Abraham Kuyper gave the Reformed churches in The
Netherlands inspired and solid leadership over many years.
Their influence traveled abroad as well. Throughout his years of
service in Christ's church and kingdom R.B. Kuiper would
always speak of Herman Bavinck with genuine and warm appreciation.

Such was the colorful and lively scene as the life of Rienk
Bouke Kuiper began to take shape in those first five years. It was
not a dull uninteresting scene, as the small village setting might
suggest. Rather it was one of bright colors and strong tones. The
father with the clear mind and the penetrating eyes and the
mother with the laughing eyes mediated those bright and strong
hues to their growing family. From that setting emerged sons
and a daughter with rich gifts for leadership and service—in the
church, in education, in business, in youth work. Those gifts
would shine most brightly in the child born in 1886.

Dominee and Mevrouw Klaas Kuiper with seven of their eight children in front
of parsonage in Garrelsweer.

Chapter 2

The New World

The list of cabin-passengers on board the steamship Maasdam sailing from Rotterdam for New York on May 23, 1891 shows the names of two Reformed ministers and their families. The name of the one minister is Rev. J.M. Remein, who had accepted a call to become pastor of the Christian Reformed Church at Rochester, New York. He is listed with his wife and eight children.

The other Reformed minister named on the passenger list is Rev. K. Kuiper. He too is listed with his wife and their eight children. The names of the eight children, given in the order of their birth, appear as follows: Mast. Barend Kuiper, Miss Rompje R. Kuiper, Miss Luberdina Kuiper, Miss Anske Kuiper, Mast. Johannes Kuiper, Mast. Rienk B. Kuiper, Mast. Hendrik Kuiper and Mast. Herman Kuiper. The listing "Miss Anske Kuiper" is amusing. Anske was a boy (later named Anton). The person responsible for the listing obviously took the name Anske to refer to a girl.

Thus after serving three Christian Reformed Churches in The Netherlands over a period of fifteen years, Dominee Klaas Kuiper, now fifty years old, accepted the call to become pastor of the First Christian Reformed Church at Grand Haven, Michigan, in the United States of America. What a momentous decision—to leave his beloved homeland where he held a position of honor and respect in order to go to a wholly new and different world where so much that was unknown awaited him and his family. Of course, since he was a lad he had known about the groups of emigrants who took the big step under the leadership of the Secession preachers A.C. Van Raalte and H.P. Scholte in

17

1846 and 1847. And he most likely read a number of letters written by another Rev. Kuiper and published as a book ten years earlier under the title *A Voice Out of America About America*.[1] Rev. Roelf T. Kuiper had come to America in 1879 and in the letters, written mainly for the benefit of prospective emigrants, he encouraged emigration. He sought to give an honest picture of conditions in the United States in 1881. He suggested that young people would have more opportunities in America, a factor which also influenced Klaas Kuiper, especially with respect to his six sons.

Rev. K. Kuiper was a sturdy man of God. He understood fully that the lives of people are governed and directed by God's wise, loving and sovereign providence. So with much prayer and soul-searching he took the big step in the conviction that the call from Grand Haven was God's call to him. This assurance prevailed through all the pangs of uncertainty, and the process of decision-making turned to high anticipation and excitement as the family embarked on its journey to a new world.

The ocean voyage on the Maasdam was largely uneventful and at times tedious. The parents were kept busy looking after their lively family on shipboard. Two incidents of interest can be related in connection with the arrival of the Kuiper family in the U.S.A. Disembarkation took place at Hoboken, New Jersey, at the docks of the Netherlands America Steam Navigation Company.[2] The Kuiper children spotted two very dark-skinned babies. This was a wholly new race of people for them and they found the black children fascinating. They couldn't draw their eyes away from the black tots until Mother Kuiper ordered them to stop staring at the little strangers.

Son Barend was now thirteen years old. He had studied English in the gymnasium (grammar school preparatory to entering the university), and he was expected to be of help in coping with language problems as the family made its way from Hoboken to Grand Haven. But Barend didn't perform too well. Father Kuiper was annoyed with his son, and scolded him for not making better use of what he had learned. Perhaps the father wasn't fully sensitive to the difference between the English of a foreign classroom and the language spoken in Hoboken.

Grand Haven, Michigan

Grand Haven, located on the eastern shore of beautiful Lake Michigan, was a delightful place for the Kuiper family to settle in the new world. For the family just come from Holland, to live in Grand Haven was to live by the sea, by one of the seas of sweet water, as the Indians called the Great Lakes. Steamboats docking at Grand Haven carried passengers to places like the great city of Chicago. The wooded dunes along the lake gave the children plenty of space to roam and to conceive marvelous things. Surely Father Kuiper, as he led his family in their daily devotions, could thank the gracious Lord for leading them into a good and pleasant land, just as He had once led His people Israel to the good land of Canaan.

Naturally there were plenty of adjustments to be made. Rienk and his brothers did not find quick social acceptance. The other boys looked upon them as foreigners, and they called the Kuiper youngsters *Dutchies*. Things were not too difficult for the new Dominie (spelled Dominee in The Netherlands). All the preaching was done in the language of his native land, as was the official work of the church. As late as 1920 the proceedings of the synods of the Christian Reformed Church were rendered almost entirely in the Dutch language. First Church itself was well established, having been organized twenty-five years earlier. A second church had been organized in 1882. So there was a sizable Christian Reformed community in the Grand Haven area when the Kuipers arrived in 1891.

Klaas Kuiper did have some trouble adjusting to the great difference between his professional and social position as a pastor in America and that which he had enjoyed in Holland. In his book *A Voice From America About America* Rev. Roelf T. Kuiper had written about the difference as follows: "Life is more roomy here, freer, easier, more common; there is more open-heartedness. Here there are few restricting and oppressive laws, rules, regulations and orders. There are far fewer formalities and rules of conduct. Everyone associates on a more equal level. True, everyone is called 'mister,' but no one 'sir,' with the exception of the preacher, who is still addressed as 'Dominie.' But no one removes his hat for him" (pp. 64ff.).

Klaas Kuiper, like Roelf T. Kuiper before him, soon came to prefer the American social ways over those in Holland so far as his own status was concerned. He made a visit to Holland just a few years after his emigration. When on his return he was asked about conditions in his former homeland he replied that he didn't like the marked class distinctions there. The K. Kuiper family was fast becoming part of America.

Christian School

It has already been stated that the preaching and official work were carried on in the Dutch language. The same was true of the local Christian school, which the Kuiper children attended. The school had been in existence for eleven years by the time the Kuiper family came on the scene. As to the instruction given there we can be best informed by one who sat under that instruction, namely, R.B. Kuiper himself. He has described that Grand Haven Christian school as follows:

> Already at that time . . . there was a Christian school in Grand Haven. That is to say, I am practically certain it was a Christian school, but I am altogether certain it was a Dutch school. We were instructed in the history of brave little Holland, not of the United States. We were taught the geography of the eleven provinces of the Netherlands, not the geography of this country. To be exact, though, I must say that we were taught the geography of Ottawa County and even went a few miles beyond it to the city of Grand Rapids. I must also add that under the progressive leadership of that pioneer of Christian education in America, B.J. Bennink, some English was soon introduced into the curriculum. By the time we left Grand Haven half a day a week was devoted to the study of the English language.[3]

An account of R.B. Kuiper's early schooling must include reference to a game he and his brothers learned to play. It is called "playing hooky," a popular slang expression conveying the pleasure of being absent from school without permission so as to enjoy something most inviting, like the water of Lake Michigan sparkling in the spring sunshine, or the dunes with flowers and trees coming back to life or in bright regalia on a day in Indian summer. When recalling those bewitching experiences R.B. always spoke of "playing hooky;" the word truant was much too stuffy for him. On one occasion he and brother John (Johannes), having stayed out of school in the afternoon, most unexpectedly met the principal after school hours as they were coming over the crest of a hill. For a moment they were paralyzed, and then ran off as fast as they could. The next day the principal told the boys that he had learned something really remarkable about them. He was accustomed to seeing them walking at a lazy pace, but now he knew they were capable of running almost as fast as a deer.

A Gifted Father

Rienk and his siblings sat under the preaching of a father whose pulpit work has been aptly described by one of the sons at the time of Klaas Kuiper's retirement in 1919. "He was a powerful preacher," Barend wrote, and his sermons were "free from one-sidedness . . . not aridly intellectualistic, nor were they excessively mystical or practical. All three elements had their rightful place in his preaching."[4] As a child Klaas Kuiper had sometimes preached to a group of his peers, and some people called him "Klaas Dominee." He told of preaching "in his thoughts" when he herded the cattle to and from pasture on his father's farm. In America the competence of the immigrant preacher was recognized, as evidenced by the inclusion of three of his sermons in a 1903 publication containing fifty-two sermons by twenty-five Christian Reformed ministers.[5]

Klaas Kuiper soon came to be known as a man with intellectual gifts and qualities of leadership. In 1893, just two years after his coming to the United States of America, he was appointed to teach four hours a week in the Theological School for one year. This was one of four interim appointments the Curatorium made to strengthen a teaching staff which, already inadequate, had been further reduced by the departure of Dr. Geerhardus Vos, brilliant biblical scholar who had accepted an appointment to teach at his alma mater, Princeton Theological Seminary. In 1894 Klaas Kuiper was elected president of the synod, broadest assembly of the Christian Reformed Church.

He was regarded as a man of mature wisdom and good counsel. R.B. Kuiper has told us that at the age of seven he accompanied his father to Grand Rapids to be present at the dedication of the new theological school building at the corner of Franklin Street and Madison Avenue (then called Fifth Avenue). Father Kuiper was then member of the Curatorium (later called Board of Trustees), a position he held for eighteen years.

Klaas Kuiper gained wide recognition and appreciation because of his weekly exposition of the Sunday School lesson. This was done over a period of twenty-five years in *The Sunday School Messenger*, a publication out of Paterson, New Jersey. Its Dutch name was *De Sabbathschool Bode*.

Leader in Education

It was especially in the broader field of Christian schooling that Klaas Kuiper quickly moved to the forefront. Just one year after coming to Grand Haven he led in the formation of a Society for Christian Instruction on Reformed Principles, an organization embracing some ten or twelve schools. Kuiper was its first president. It appears that devotion to the Christian day school was lagging. But the cause did have its loyal friends. Writing about the situation prevailing toward the end of the century, Richard Postma, longtime leader in the Christian School movement, had this to say: "Happily these few friends were not without spokesmen. There were in those days some active and able propagandists and among them the Rev. K. Kuiper undoubtedly held first place."[6]

In the name of the society founded under Kuiper's leadership the words "on Reformed principles" are of critical importance. They were such to Klaas Kuiper, and certainly were not an expression of a narrow Dutch or parochial point of view. For him to be Christian meant to be Reformed, Calvinistic. For this reason he was not at all impressed by the repeated arguments of those who held that separate Christian schools were not needed. Christians could control the public schools in communities dominated by Christians, so the argument ran, and in doing so the public school could be "saved." Kuiper's reply was simply, "For our own children do we demand instruction given according to Reformed principles."[7] It was his driving conviction that the Christian school was absolutely essential for the preservation of the spiritual identity of a Reformed people. That his conception of Reformed principles had depth is fully apparent from a sermon by him on the words of I Samuel 2:3b—"The Lord is God of all knowledge."[8]

The leadership of this man was so effective because it was always clear-minded and sharply focused, as was that of his most celebrated son after him. He always spoke and wrote with a sure sense of where he stood and where he wanted to go. Take, for example, an action taken at the first meeting of the society founded in 1892 and over which he presided. A resolution was passed recommending that Christian schools should be parent-society controlled; they should not be parochial.[9] The earlier schools among the Christian Reformed people in America were parochial, that is, operated and controlled by the local organized church. K. Kuiper had learned his Reformed principles well under the tutelage of Abraham Kuyper. General education belongs in the sovereign sphere of the family, not in that of the organized church (nor, of course, in the sovereign sphere of the state).

As Klaas Kuiper gave sound and aggressive leadership to the Christian school movement, he began to agitate for improved education at higher levels. He saw that the higher educational setup maintained in Grand Rapids by the Christian Reformed Churches was far from adequate. The centerpiece of that program was the Theological School for the training of ministers of the gospel, and connected with the Theological School was a Literary Department, which was in fact little more than a senior high school. So the sharp-eyed immigrant pastor from Grand Haven issued a call that soon began to ring as a challenge throughout the Christian Reformed Church—"There must be a college." It is significant that the very synod at which Rev. Klaas Kuiper presided action was taken that opened the way to the development of Calvin College. The Synod of 1894 decided that "also those who do not wish to be prepared for the ministry, may be admitted to studies in the Literary Department."[10] From that tiny seed a college did grow, slowly, as it was not until 1920 that a college as a distinct institution was in operation, with the first A.B. degrees granted in 1921. The

college, which would in time come to be recognized as one of the
nation's finest smaller colleges, owes much to the preacher who
persisted in his challenging call for a college.

The contributions of Rev. K. Kuiper in the area of Christian
education have been pointedly described by Rev. Wm. Stuart, a
colleague of K. Kuiper in Roseland (Chicago) and a teacher of
Bible for many years in the Grand Rapids Christian High
School. At the time of K. Kuiper's death in 1921 Stuart wrote as
follows:

> Rev. K. Kuiper was a man of significance for our churches . . .
> The Christian school had the love of his heart, and by spoken
> word and pen he labored tirelessly until even the very latest
> struggle involving the Christian school. I would almost call
> him the father of Christian education. He was privileged to see
> that instruction come to full flower, also in the development of
> the Christian high schools. But already years ago he went far-
> ther in his zeal for a college, and he also lived to see a college
> come to full growth. It is difficult to express in words how
> much the churches owe him for his constant and urgent
> pleading, as he persisted in declaring, "There must be a col-
> lege."[11]

Kuiper's splendid contributions to the cause of Christian
education, education "on Reformed principles," are reflected
not only in the growth of schools at all levels, but also in the contributions his children would make to the cause that the father
promoted so avidly. Already in 1903 the firstborn son Barend
joined his voice to that of his father by writing a small book entitled *The Proposed Calvinistic College in Grand Rapids*. The
book pleaded for the development of a true center of learning
that would rise above the limitations of a denominational college.[12] Son Rienk would become president of Calvin College and
later of Calvin Seminary. Two sons (Barend and Herman) would
serve as professors in Calvin Seminary, with Barend gaining a
reputation as a superb teacher of church history. Son Henry
would be one of three co-founders in 1920 of the National Union
of Christian Schools (today named Christian Schools International). To complete the family circle we note that daughter
Luberdina (called Tante Dena by the nephews and nieces) also
worked with young people but not in formal education. For
many years she filled a leadership role in the American Federa-

tion of Reformed Young Women's Societies, a forerunner of the Young Calvinist organization.

The five years that the Klaas Kuiper family spent in Grand Haven were, it is evident, years filled with growth and service. The older children were reaching maturity. The manse at First Church was alive with those numberless activities, sounds and expectations that come with such a growing family. But it was not all bubbling livelines. One of the children, Rompje (Rolena), had never been well. Slowly her health failed, until the dark cloud of sorrow settled on the parsonage when the second-born child died in the autumn of 1893. Her remains were interred in what became a family burial plot under the trees amid the dunes that rest peacefully along the shore of beautiful Lake Michigan.

Chapter 3

Chicago

As we have seen when Rienk Bouke Kuiper was five years old the Klaas Kuiper family moved from the Dutch village of Garrelsweer to the growing American town of Grand Haven, Michigan. That move was a momentous one. Almost equally so was the next move. When Rienk was ten years old the family moved to the big, booming city of Chicago. Rev. K. Kuiper accepted the call from the Second Christian Reformed Church of Roseland to become their pastor. Rienk was not part of a family that was afraid to take big steps.

Chicago was on the move in those days. Its population growth between the Civil War and the World War has been described as staggering. This was due largely to immigration. Waves of newcomers settled in ethnically friendly enclaves throughout the city. Started as a town with three hundred fifty inhabitants in 1833, the city had passed the one million mark by 1896. Many Hollanders came too. A University of Chicago study published in 1903 revealed that there were in Chicago thirty-five thousand people speaking the Dutch language, and that there were more Hollanders here than in any other American city, with Grand Rapids second and Paterson third. In 1896 there were among the Dutch-speaking people three congregations of the Christian Reformed Church in Chicago proper, and six congregations of the Reformed Church in America.

This city on the move had its own character. There was a brash spirit of doing big things. The city had done a remarkable job of rebuilding after the disastrous fire twenty-five years before. Here was the railroad center of the nation; business and industry roared. The World's Columbian Exposition in 1893 had attracted global attention to this vigorous young giant among American cities. Men with names like McCormick, Pullman, Swift, Field and Harper were moving the city forward at a fast pace. The special character of this dynamic city has been caught by Illinois' own poet Carl Sandburg in his "Chicago"—

> Hog Butcher for the World,
> Tool Maker, Stacker of Wheat,
> Player with Railroads and the Nation's Freight Handler;
> Stormy, husky, brawling,
> City of the Big Shoulders.

This city would be home base for the Kuiper family for fifteen years. So it was in Chicago that sails were set in the lives of the growing children and young people. Inevitably these developing lives were significantly influenced by this dynamic, materialistic environment. A sharpened awareness of their spiritual roots together with a certain toughness of character would be necessary in order to maintain a sense of identity in this cultural whirl. In all but one of the children the solid spiritual anchorage of their lives held firm. Two sons entered business. One (Johannes—John) became a gracious Christian gentleman, active in Christ's kingdom as he was successful in the retail food business. The other son (Anton) became a prosperous insurance broker with offices in the Loop. He drifted away from the church, much to the sorrow of the rest of the family. Near the end of Father Kuiper's days he wrote one final tender letter to his wayward son, pleading with him to return to the faith of his fathers and to make peace with the Savior. Anton did not heed the plea. As he neared death in 1937, a member of the family visited him and offered to pray with him. "Make it short," was his curt response.

Student Robert Kuiper

The Roseland School for Christian Instruction began in a small way in 1891. A lot of hard work by dedicated people launched and maintained the school. On coming to Chicago Klaas Kuiper promptly gave his vigorous support to the cause.

In an address delivered soon after his arrival there he spoke as follows: "We are deeply convinced that it is the duty of all those who with us confess the Reformed principles to stand shoulder to shoulder with us in the struggle against unbelief to the end that our children may be instructed in accord with these principles."[1] The record shows that in July of 1896 this forward-looking man, an immigrant only five years before, advocated instruction in both English and Dutch in the school.[2]

R.B. Kuiper has spoken of his experience in the Roseland school in these words: "In 1896 we moved to Chicago. We boys attended the Christian School on 104th Street. If ever there was a Dutch school on this continent, that was it. Believe it or not, we were taught arithmetic from books imported from the old country. And so at the age of ten I knew almost all about the metric system—meters, liters, grams, etc.—but I learned subsequently in a public school that there are twelve inches to a foot, four quarts in a gallon, and two thousand pounds in a ton."[3]

Just when Rienk came to be known as Robert is not clear. It may have been at the time of the move to Chicago, although more than likely it was at the time he enrolled in the Van Vlissingen public school for the ninth grade.[4] The name Rienk would have sounded very odd to the pupils at Van Vlissingen. He was known as Robert Kuiper throughout his high school years. And the diploma he received from the University of Chicago after two years there, granting him the Associate in Arts degree, has the name Robert Kuiper inscribed on it. But the name Rienk Kuiper appears on his diploma at the time he received his A.B. degree from the University. At times he was also called "Bill." More than once I have heard relatives call him, "Uncle Rob" or "Uncle Bill."

Wherever he went to school Rienk (Robert) distinguished himself as a superior student. His grades were always high. While at the Van Vlissingen school he won an award for an essay on the subject "Santa Claus and Christmas in the Netherlands" in an annual Christmas Story competition sponsored by the *Chicago Record*. While at this school he also wrote an essay on "American Patriotism." It is still good reading, not only for its thoughtful content, but also because it is done in excellent penmanship and with a regard for grammatical and linguistic accuracy that would put many contemporary high school graduates to shame. One paragraph of the essay points to the city in which it was written. "When anybody stuffs the ballot," said Robert, "he shows that he has not love for his country at all, and that he is a cheater. This act can be performed in a great many different manners. One of the most common ways is to vote at more than one polling place." The young patriot felt that all citizens should strive to keep the streets clean. "In this city," he went on, "where so very few clean streets can be found, we have a good chance to show our patriotism in this way." He reveals his Dutch rearing not only in an occasional "Dutchism" in his writing but also when he adds, "But we should not forget to keep our homes clean."

R.B. at ten (right).

From Van Vlissingen Robert went to the Morgan Park
Military Academy, at that time part of the University of Chicago
academic program. The Chicago Christian High School was
then not yet in existence. Morgan Park Academy was located
about two and one-half miles from the Kuiper home, and
Robert walked the five mile round trip every school day. Here
again he did superior work. He held an Academy scholarship
each of the three years he attended the school, and on graduation in 1903 he was awarded a Morgan Park Academy scholarship for entrance at the University of Chicago. Years later a
classmate dropped a card to R.B. Kuiper reflecting on their student days at the Academy, saying, "You may not remember me,
but if you hadn't loaned me your Latin notes I probably would
not have graduated . . . You've gone far—no wonder. You were
the smartest lad in our class." One of R.B.'s reminiscences of
his school days at the Academy was that he experienced more
than a little embarrassment there because he had only one good
suit to wear at proper occasions, while most of the students had
a much more ample wardrobe.

Work and Fun

The story of R.B. Kuiper's Chicago years is not just one of
books and excellent schoolwork. It is also a story of work done
in order to help meet the living costs of this large family. Robert
and his brothers often worked in the produce fields of south
Chicago. They earned twenty-five cents a day for this back-
straining work, work which seems often to have been that of
picking onions. Robert also worked in the shops of the great
Pullman company, a workplace not without its dangers due to
the hot rivets being tossed about. Thus the plain working people
of the world were not distant folk to him, nor were they mere
social statistics. He was part of them. He would always feel comfortable with such people. At the same time, because his experience with the humble working folk was in the big city, he
developed an earthy, street-wise sharpness that would stand him
in good stead in dealing with complex issues. Although his
achievements as a scholar were impressive, he would never be
nor could he be an ivory tower academic. A friend of mine has

told me that when R.B. was college president he stopped one day to chat with him and his companion as they were digging a trench for a city utility. The president's demeanor was not at all patronizing or stand-offish, but was simple, direct and genuine, exhibiting a sincere interest in the job the two young men were doing. His speech would always be direct and crystal clear. He never dangled his meanings tauntingly from skyhooks of fancy words and beautiful but vague phrases. His Chicago years show up in an expression he sometimes used to sharpen a discussion, the words "Let's call a spade a spade."

The story of R.B.'s Chicago years is also a story of fun and laughter. How could it be otherwise with this family of six bright boys. And they were real boys. R.B. always spoke of "sissies" with contempt. The boys had to be a bit cautious in what they did because there was sister Dena. Being older than most of the boys, she felt some responsibility for their behavior. One day Robert and a brother were on south Michigan Avenue playing the game of hooky and blithely licking five-cent ice cream cones. How delightfully carefree they were, with the chores of schoolwork far from their thoughts. Suddenly their bliss turned into deep despair. Whom should they meet but sister Dena. They knew only too well what that would mean when they returned home. Their painful expectations were not disappointed, and they got a good licking from Pa.

On another occasion when Robert and a brother were playing that special game they stopped at a high wooden fence. They discovered a knothole and peeped through it to see what might be behind the fence. As they were peering through the hole a hand mysteriously came over the top of the fence and took the cap off the head of one of the boys. The cap disappeared over the top of the fence. The boys were thoroughly shaken. Feeling guilty about their unlawful absence from school, they came to the disturbing conclusion that the "person" who reached over that high fence was most surely the devil himself. As they hung around for a while, wondering what to do in their weird experience with the evil one, the cap suddenly came back over the fence. On returning home they did not report their encounter with Satan.

The boys became rather innovative and daring in another one of their escapades. With time on their hands one pleasant summer day, Robert and two of his brothers hit upon a scheme that mesmerized them with its possibilities. They decided that they would act as a committee of three to deliver a message from their father to a member of the congregation. Why they chose the man they did is unknown. Their message was simple: Pa wanted to see him. The man was obviously puzzled, but did not question the authenticity of the call from his pastor. So the parishioner made his way to the parsonage and was admitted by Mrs. Kuiper as he told her that Dominie wanted to see him. The pastor welcomed the member of his flock and asked him to sit down. Then there was an awkward period of silence as they looked at each other. The visitor assumed the pastor would promptly tell him why he wanted to see him, and the pastor expected the man to announce what he had on his mind. Finally the visitor said that Dominie wanted to see him. Pastor Kuiper in turn said that he was glad to see the member of his congregation, but he had no special reason to expect him. Then it was disclosed that the pastor's three boys had been at the man's home with a message from their father. So that was it. Three sad boys were soon on their way for a second visit to the man's home, this time with a sheepish apology, part of the discipline meted out by their father.

The cultural advantages of the big city were not neglected—such as the new Field Museum of Natural History, the Art Institute and the Chicago Symphony Orchestra. The first visit at a concert by the orchestra was spoiled for the boys in a manner they had not anticipated. The beautiful and stirring music in the concert hall setting with all the attendant excitement was a bit much for sister Dena and she cried through most of the performance, much to the boys' disgust.

University of Chicago

Rienk entered upon a new and stimulating chapter of his life in the autumn of 1903 when he enrolled at the University of Chicago. Barend, we have noted, was a student there before him. Father Kuiper, known for his persistent call for a college true to the faith, did not feel that the Literary Department associated with the Theological School in Grand Rapids, was adequate for his boys with their aptitude for fruitful study and with an excellent high school education at the Morgan Park Academy already behind them. In addition to Barend and Rienk brother Herman also attended the university.

The University of Chicago was an exciting place, mainly because of the remarkable man who was its first president, and also because of the group of first-rate scholars that he gathered around him. William Rainey Harper[5] was a rare individual with immense learning, seemingly unlimited energy, and an extraordinary capacity to get people to do what he wanted them to do. This amazing person had entered Muskingum College in Ohio at the age of ten, was graduated at the age of thirteen. His exceptional intelligence was coupled with boundless enthusiasm. He chose to study Hebrew. At sixteen he was a college teacher of elementary Hebrew. He was offered the position of tutor in the preparatory department of an Ohio university. His field was Latin and Greek, but before long he had a class in Hebrew, which was attended at first mostly by professors and then by large numbers of undergraduates. In time this man was teaching classes in Hebrew at many different locations and also by way of correspondence, with literally thousands of students enthusiastically pursuing a subject that most people thought was of interest only to a handful of scholars. Through an extraordinary confluence of circumstances together with Harper's astounding capacity for hard work and his hypnotic ability to persuade people his dream of a "great university" was realized when the school opened its doors in 1892—in Chicago, "of all places," said the Boston *Post* as it echoed the scorn of the east for the cultural wasteland that the brash city on Lake Michigan was in the eyes of many in that part of the country.

Harper's infectious enthusiasm coupled with his native shrewdness enabled him to obtain millions of dollars for his Chicago dream from America's leading financier, John D. Rockefeller—a rare feat in view of Rockefeller's realistic and hard-nosed response to requests for his money. Harper not only gathered lots of money for his project; he also gathered an outstanding group of leading scholars for the building of an impressive faculty. Many a celebrated eastern university or college lost irreplaceable people to "Harper's folly" in Chicago. Harper offered these scholars a top salary of $6000 to $7000 a year, which was double the prevailing wage in the academic world. Among those who succumbed to Harper's persuasive overtures was Paul Shorey of Bryn Mawr, reputed to be America's leading Greek scholar at the time. Another famous name gracing the Greek-teaching faculty was Edgar J. Goodspeed, who gained wide recognition for his own translation of the Greek New Testament. Rienk Bouke Kuiper's academic record at the University of Chicago contains this notice: Honors in Greek. These honors under such teaching meant much.

This university with its celebrated president and faculty was ideally suited for R.B.'s pursuit of his college career. The enthusiasm for learning that Harper inspired permeated the education given at this newcomer among American universities. The high level of competence of the faculty challenged Rienk's active mind to give its best. Under Harper the university was divided into the academic college for the first two years and the university college for the last two years. The first two years were given to general education and the last two to specialization. This arrangement had much to do with the development of the Junior College movement in the country. Accordingly, as already mentioned, Robert Kuiper received a diploma after two years, a diploma signed by William Rainey Harper. The illustrious first president did not sign Rienk's diploma after four years of schooling. Harper died of cancer in 1905 at the age of forty-nine.

Throughout his four years at the university Rienk Bouke Kuiper distinguished himself as a first-rate scholar. His achievements were recognized when, already at the end of his third year, he was chosen to membership in the nation's top academic society, the Phi Beta Kappa fraternity. R.B. was always justifiably proud of his Phi Beta Kappa key as it hung from the watch chain running across his vest. And when he completed his course at Chicago in 1907, these words were placed next to his name in the school annual *Cap and Gown*, "His daily food is honors; his daily drink is praise."

Chapter 4

Preacher in Training

What should he do with his life? R.B. Kuiper knew well enough that he wanted to spend his life in the service of God and to His glory. That had been well drilled into his soul by his father with his unrelenting emphasis on "Reformed principles." That did not, of course, settle all questions. What specific work should he do? The options that beckoned him were two, namely, a career as a teacher or as a preacher.

This question was unsettled when he completed his work at the University of Chicago. And this large question was still on his mind when he attended the University of Indiana for a year of graduate study with his major in Latin. With the superior teaching he had received at Chicago in the classical languages, a year of graduate study in Latin would amply qualify him to teach Latin or Greek or both. Of course, such graduate study would be useful too in the study of theology with its basically Latinate vocabulary.

So he was not simply marking time at Bloomington, Indiana, for a year. Again he did what he had always done as a student; he gave his best and again gained recognition as a top-notch scholar. In a letter of recommendation the professor in charge of the Department of Comparative Philology at the University of Indiana wrote as follows about his student, "Mr. Kuiper did his work thoroughly and with accuracy and judgment . . . I do not hesitate to say that Mr. Kuiper is one of the most scholarly young men it has been my pleasure to work with."

The letter of recommendation, written at R.B.'s request, was accompanied by a personal note. In this personal communication, dated August 17, 1908, Professor G.H. Stempel

35

said, "I'm glad to note you are going on with your studies. You have the making of a scholar and a college teacher . . ." At the end of his letter the Indiana professor referred to time spent in the Chicago area recently and then added, "At another time I hope to see something of the University and to renew acquaintance with you." From this it would appear that Professor Stempel thought R.B. Kuiper was planning to continue his studies in classical languages at the University of Chicago. This was, we noted, after the middle of August in 1908.

Just what took place in R.B. Kuiper's mind at that time we do not know. It seems reasonable to assume that he did not arrive at a decision at this crucial point in his life without some struggle. Many a former student of his, I among them, can testify to the sympathy and understanding with which R.B. dealt with them under similar circumstances in their lives. Whatever may have been the wrestlings that took place in his life at the time, the outcome was that in September of 1908 R.B. Kuiper was enrolled in the denominational Theological School in Grand Rapids. The church of Jesus Christ has much reason for gratitude that the Holy Spirit in His own way and seemingly at a late hour snatched this highly gifted man for service in a career that so admirably suited the talents with which he had been endowed. So R.B. returned as a student to the building whose dedication he had witnessed with his father at the age of seven and where his brother B.K. was a teacher in the Literary Department.

Theological School

What did R.B. Kuiper think as he entered upon a three-year course of study in which almost all of the teaching was in the Dutch language, after his years of study at Morgan Park, Chicago and Indiana? A check on the class notes taken by R.B. reveals that seemingly only one course that he took was given in English. This was a course in New Testament Greek taught by Professor L. Berkhof. Also, when he entered the school in Grand Rapids, R.B. had the benefit of an education quite superior to that of most of his fellow students.[1] He had no difficulty maintaining his record as an outstanding student. He taught a course in speech in the Literary Department. The student body of the Theological School numbered thirty-one in R.B.'s middler (second) year. Four professors comprised the faculty at that time. They were Louis Berkhof, Gabriel D. De Jong, William Heyns and Foppe M. Ten Hoor.

At the time of the writing of this book only one person survives who was a student at the Theological School when R.B. was there. He is Rev. Henry Baker, highly respected minister in the Christian Reformed Church who had reached the grand old age of ninety-seven years. His hearing was impaired but his mind was still clear when I spoke with him about his student days at the Theological School. "Oh yes, I remember R.B. Kuiper very well. Everybody knew R.B. We called him R.B. He was a very good student, a very good student," Rev. Baker reflected. And then he added, "He had a lot of ability, you know." The high regard R.B. Kuiper enjoyed as a student at the Theological School was demonstrated by the honor bestowed on him at the end of his days at the school. He was chosen to give the commencement address at the time of his graduation. At that time it was customary to choose a member of the graduating class to carry out this special function. When in 1956 R.B. gave the commencement address at Calvin College and Seminary for

R.B. in Theological School (back row, third from left).

The Theological School graduate.

the fourth time (when college and seminary still had a joint commencement), he suggested that the old custom be revived, and then he added with customary wry humor, "One never knows more than at the time of one's graduation."

In the years that I was part of the inner family circle I very rarely heard R.B. speak of his years at the Theological School. Not very much specific information is available about that epoch in his life. However, we do know of certain questions which commanded the attention of the church at that time. R.B. came from a home where there had always been an avid interest in matters of concern in the church and in theology. An age of preoccupation with television and sports finds it hard to believe that R.B. as a growing youth found satisfaction in listening in on many a spirited debate on a certain weighty theological issue among ministers gathered in the parsonage. Debate on this very issue increased when R.B. entered the Theological School in 1908.[2] This issue was the infra-supra question, a question unique to Reformed theology with its teaching of predestination. It is an intriguing question, but not a popular one. It is too profound to be popular.[3] In later years R.B. sometimes remarked, with a hint of a grin on his face, that at the time of his marriage some people wondered how he with his infralapsarian bent of mind could take to himself a mate who held to the supralapsarian view. It was hard to tell at such times whether he was serious or joking, but it was not apparent that differences over this arcane theological question had any unsettling effect on their marriage.

The Seminary and the Church

A much less obscure question occupying the mind of the church at that time had to do with the relationship between the church and the Theological School. Does the church have authority over the education of its future ministers? R.B. would become much involved with this question at a later time. Professor Ten Hoor was sure that the answer to this question was in the affirmative. Others were not so sure. In 1906 the synod of the Christian Reformed Church appointed a committee to study this question and a related one. In 1908 the synod referred the matter to the consistories of the churches for their reaction. In

1910, when R.B. had completed two years at the Theological School, synod received some fifteen overtures on the question, with opinions divided on the issue. The synod's decision was to accept the situation as it prevailed at the time. "But did not express itself regarding the principles involved. Opinions as to these principles differed and do differ still," a former professor at the school stated in 1926.[4]

The very same issue came up again some years later under the heading of "Free Study." An overture from the LaGrave Avenue Christian Reformed Church (of which R.B. was pastor at the time) asked that exceptions be allowed to the church's rule that a student seeking to be a minister and who had studied elsewhere must spend his last year at the Theological School of the church. A committee to examine the principle of "free study" was appointed, with R.B. Kuiper one of the five members. Dr. Cornelius Van Til, then pastor at Spring Lake, Michigan, was also a member of the committee. The committee, reporting in 1932, recommended that the church recognize the principle of "free study," but also recommended that the church enforce the general rule requiring its future ministers to take their last year of study at Calvin Seminary,[5] with the Board of Trustees given power to allow for exceptions under "extraordinary circumstances." After much discussion synod decided to table the whole matter. Thus the church did not express itself on the principles involved.[6]

Bull sessions in which current issues were discussed together with the daily grind of studying Hebrew, Greek and theology were not the only matters filling the life of a theological student. There were also the occasions when the student was called upon to exercise his skills in exhorting in some pulpit. The students were properly told that they did not *preach* until they were duly ordained. As students they *exhorted*. R.B. was very nervous when he exhorted for the first time. The hostess at whose home he was guest prepared a delicious dinner, but he was too nervous to eat. He distinctly sensed that his hostess felt hurt at his failure to enjoy the good things she had prepared, and ever after he was uncomfortable when he recalled his miserable performance as guest at that Sunday dinner.

Romance

And then there was romance to sweeten the steady diet of Hebrew and Greek and theology. In R.B.'s student days the Theological School was much like a monastery. The married student was an exception. But there was romance as the young men courted their prospective manse partners. R.B. met an attractive and competent schoolteacher in Grand Rapids. She was principal of the West Side Christian School. Her name was Marie Janssen. A former pupil told me of times when she was asked to keep an eye on the class while Miss Janssen stepped outside to greet her calling suitor. Miss Janssen came from a Zeeland, Michigan, farm family that knew something about advanced education. Marie's brother Ralph earned a Ph.D. degree in Germany and taught at the Theological School in Grand Rapids from 1902 to 1906. Ralph Janssen returned to the theological faculty in 1914 and became the central figure in a celebrated controversy. This subject will be discussed in a subsequent chapter.

Marie Janssen became the bride of R.B. Kuiper very soon after he finished his studies at the Theological School. According to the announcement sent out by the widowed mother, Mrs. J. Janssen, daughter "Maria" was married to Rienk B. Kuiper on Sunday evening at 7:30 o'clock on June 18, 1911, at the First Christian Reformed Church of Zeeland. The wedding was part of the regular evening worship service. This beginning of the marriage in God's house in the fellowship of the saints at worship was a good beginning of a fruitful union in which Rienk and Marie worked together most effectively in Christ's kingdom for almost fifty-five years. A more trivial but interesting detail of the wedding was that the bride and groom arrived at and left the church in an automobile—a rare bit of class in Zeeland in 1911.

Many years later R.B. made reference to his marriage to Marie Janssen in an article he wrote for the seventy-fifth anniversary booklet of the West Side Christian School. In his inimitable manner he said in 1958, "Some forty-eight years ago I did the West Side Christian School a great disservice. I robbed them of a very able principal—Miss Marie Janssen. How gracious of the editors of the anniversary book to ask me for a contribution! I appreciate their forgiving spirit and hope at this late date to make some restitution, be it ever so slight."

Princeton Seminary

As R.B. approached the end of his three years at the Theological School he was contemplating further study. In the

R.B. and his bride.

spring of 1911 he inquired about the possibilities for advanced study at the Glasgow College of the Free Church of Scotland, a school where the names of Professors James Orr and James Denney were prominent. The response R.B. received from James Denney did not satisfy him. What other inquiries he made we do not know. What we do know is that in September 1911 Mr. and Mrs. R.B. Kuiper were in Princeton, New Jersey, where R.B. had matriculated as a graduate student at the Theological Seminary of the Presbyterian Church. He was the beneficiary of a fellowship in pursuing his studies at Princeton under some of America's outstanding theologians. Although in later years R.B. most frequently spoke of the work he took under Benjamin Breckinridge Warfield, he also took courses with Caspar Wistar Hodge (son of a previous professor with the same name) and even more with Geerhardus Vos. At the end of his year there he was granted the degree of Bachelor of Divinity.

R.B.'s reputation as a scholar did not suffer at Princeton. His standing as a superior student was evidenced by the appearance of a book entitled *Is Jesus God*.[7] This publication, containing nine essays by as many students, was produced in commemoration of the centennial anniversary of the founding of Princeton Theological Seminary in 1812. In an introductory note Professor B.B. Warfield indicated that the nine essays were chosen from a "considerable number of essays" submitted. The first chapter is by Rienk B. Kuiper on the question, "Does the Christian Church Teach the Deity of Christ?" R.B.'s contribution reveals a mind capable of highly orderly thought, lucid writing and impressive logic. Sharp logic and orderly thought sparkle in the following quotation: "We must also here face the question which very naturally presents itself, Can a church that denies the deity of Christ be called Christian? It is evident that a negative answer to this question at this stage of the discussion would at once destroy the problem. For if only that Church which teaches the deity of Christ is truly Christian, then of course the Christian Church teaches the deity of Christ, or else there is no Christian Church."

When Princeton Theological Seminary held its centennial anniversary celebration in May of 1912, Professor L. Berkhof came from Grand Rapids to represent the Theological School of the Christian Reformed Church at the festive affair. In reporting on his visit to Princeton, Berkhof "made mention also of the fact that the Faculty of the Princeton Seminary considered the students of the Theological School of Grand Rapid as some of the best that follow a post-graduate course in theology at the seminary."[8] This was, of course, at the time when R.B. was a graduate student at Princeton Seminary, together with three others from the Grand Rapids school, namely, H.Henry Meeter (Professor of Bible at Calvin College from 1926 to 1956), Jacob Mulder and Gerrit Hoeksema. R.B. was offered a fellowship for study abroad after his year at Princeton, but he declined. He was now ready to become a pastor. His year of study at Princeton established his credentials among Presbyterians as a theologian and scholar. In 1929 when conservative forces in the Presbyterian Church in the U.S.A. broke away from Princeton to establish Westminster Theological Seminary in Philadelphia, R.B. Kuiper, then a Christian Reformed pastor in Grand Rapids, was called upon to become Professor of Systematic Theology.

The year at Princeton was fruitful in another way. Rienk and Marie Kuiper became parents as their first child was born on April 8, 1912. The newborn child, named Marietta Rolena, received a gift from Dr. and Mrs. B.B. Warfield along with a note which said, "Doctor and Mrs. Warfield present their compliments to little Miss Kuiper, and beg to congratulate her on being born, and to thank her for being born in Princeton. Will she kindly accept these little pins as a souvenir of her birthplace? April 9, 1912." This gracious welcome to the future wife of the writer of this book was a fitting beginning of a beautiful life.

Chapter 5

Pastor R.B. Kuiper

RINCK B. KUIPER NOW A MINISTER— these words formed
the headline over an article in the Grand Rapids daily newspaper of July 12, 1912. The faulty spelling of Rienk's name
was not the only error in the newspaper piece. It represented him
as being a graduate of Northwestern University as well as the
University of Chicago. And he was actually not yet a minister.
He still had to be ordained and installed. The article had to do
with his successful examination before Classis Zeeland two days
before. What was of special note in the article was the description of "a touching scene" when the president of the Classis
congratulated the candidate on his successful examination as
Rienk stood before the assembly with "his gray-haired father"
by his side. The newspaper call the father "this grand old man."

Overisel

Thus R.B. Kuiper passed the last test so that he could enter
upon the ministry of the Word and sacraments at Overisel,
Michigan. On Sunday morning, July 14, 1912, he was ordained
and installed in the church he was to serve. This important event
in the minister's life was conducted by his father Rev. Klaas
Kuiper, and Rev. Douwe R. Drukker, counselor to the congregation during the time it was without a pastor. That afternoon R.B. preached his first sermon as an ordained minister. He
preached on the words of Hebrews 13:8, "Jesus Christ the same
yesterday, and today, and forever." The clerk of the church
council, D. Vander Kamp, summarized the sermon as follows:

45

"He urged us to follow the faith of our pastors (Heb. 13:7), because though they themselves have departed, Jesus Christ, the object and content of their preaching, constantly remains the same, the same Son of God, the same savior of sinners. Upon him and upon nothing besides him our minister would have us steadfastly fix our eyes."[1]

Overisel is a tiny village about five miles southeast of Holland, Michigan. R.B. had five calls as he was completing his graduate studies at Princeton. They were from Christian Reformed Churches at Lucas, Michigan; New Era, Michigan; the Broadway church in Grand Rapids, and from Classis Illinois to serve as its Home Missionary—in addition to the call from Overisel. An attractive feature of the Overisel call was that it would place him less than five miles from his aging parents at Niekerk and just a bit farther from Mrs. Kuiper's people near Zeeland. We do not know how much these personal factors weighed in his consideration of the calls received.

The terms of these letters of call of the year 1912 make fascinating reading. The Grand Rapids church offered an annual salary of $1000, as did Classis Illinois. The other three churches offered $900. All the call letters are rendered in the Dutch language, but in the letter from Broadway the word "Engelsch" was added, most likely meaning that some or all of the worship services were in the English language. All the calls offered free parsonage. Then there were some special items. Lucas promised a barn, five acres of ground and free fuel. New Era offered two acres of ground for gardening. Overisel called with these perks—barn, buggy, cutter. But the pastor himself must take care of the horse, the call stipulated.

The horse was an important part of the country parson's life. His daughter remembered with pleasure riding in the buggy with her father as he ran some errand or made a call. Each week the young preacher traveled in his horse-drawn vehicle to two or three different locations at country schools to teach catechism to clusters of children of the congregation. These schools were about three or four miles from the church and parsonage. Oldsters at Overisel recall R.B. as being a strict teacher. "We had to know our stuff," one of them told me. Incidentally, if the horse's harness needed repair there was help nearby. Next door to the parsonage there was at that time a harness and shoe repair shop operated by a man the people called Smiggy. R.B. and Smiggy hit it off very well. He apparently didn't get along so well with the local pastor of the Reformed Church in America (also called the Dutch Reformed Church). Their coolness as they met on the street reflected the attitude that then prevailed between the two denominatinons.

Growing Reputation

"An outstanding preacher"—that is the reputation R.B. gained in the area. He had "good sermons," I was told. He was not a long-winded preacher. He could say what he had to say in twenty minutes or so. He worked hard on his sermons, so that he laid out the text of Scripture accurately, logically and with utmost clarity. This meant that he thought through his material to a point of complete clarity for himself. R.B.'s son Klaudius, who was born during the Overisel ministry, reports that his father always put a lot of work into his sermons. The intensity and deep earnestness with which he preached bore out the thoroughness with which the biblical message mastered him as much as he had mastered the message he brought.

His developing reputation as a preacher is revealed by two facts. In 1914 a book was published with the title *Manifold Grace*. Its subtitle *Twelf Sermons* tells something about the book's contents and about the printer's schooling in the Dutch language. The book contains sermons by eleven well-known ministers in the Christian Reformed Church in that era. Two of the sermons are by one man, M.J. Bosma. For R.B. Kuiper to be placed in this select company at so early a stage in his ministry says a great deal about what lay ahead for this promising young preacher.

Also pointing to a bright future was the quality of this sermon published so early in his career. It is most gripping in its orderly development of thought, its inescapable lucidity, and its arresting personal appeal. The sermon is entitled "Jesus Sentenced to Death On His Confession Of Himself As The Son Of God" and is based on Matthew 26:62-66. In describing the unique suffering Jesus experienced before Caiaphas and the Sanhedrin the preacher's thought progresses in cascades of sparkling truth:

Such treatment, which would have pained you and me, doubtless grieved Jesus so much more that a comparison is hardly possible. The reason for this lies in the fact that he himself was the truth. If *we* find ourselves in the presence of liars, we are not far from our proper place, for we too are liars. When *Jesus* saw himself surrounded by liars, He was as distant from his proper sphere as could be, for He is truth itself. If *we* are not always believed, that is not surprising, for as a matter of fact we cannot be fully trusted. When *Jesus* was not believed, He must have been pained grievously, for He deserves unlimited confidence. If *we* are asked to take an oath, this demand is not altogether unreasonable, for we may tell falsehoods. When *Jesus* was asked to swear an oath, this was a cruel insult because He could not lie. If *we* are charged with perjury, such is awful; yet not one of us can say that he is immune from this sin. When *Jesus* was accused of perjury, this was the hardest blow to his soul that man could strike.

Finally, let us bear in mind that it was his statement that He was God's Son that was declared perjury. The most important testimony of himself that He ever gave or could give was adjudged perjury. The grandest confession of himself that He ever made or could make was regarded perjury. This blow must have occasioned more grief to his soul than all the fist-blows that were soon to be given him, yea, than the blows which nailed him to the cross.

Can you tell me how it was possible for him to endure this suffering? to endure it so quietly, so willingly? Can you tell me how it was possible for him when He was so reviled, not to revile again? I fail to understand. But this I do know: it was his own choice, his own will, to suffer thus. And when He chose this, He thought of us. For our sakes He willed to suffer. He suffered to free us from suffering. Beloved, if his love was so great, should we not requite it with our whole heart's love?[2]

First Publication

Another publication from R.B.'s pen appeared in 1914. This first publication under R.B. Kuiper's own name was on the subject of *Christian Liberty*. Bound in a paper cover, the booklet contained a lecture given at the Theological School and Calvin College in Grand Rapids in February of 1914. Against the prevailing and increasingly secularistic notions of liberty stemming from the French Revolution R.B.'s lecture advanced the proposition "that the Christian alone is truly free."[3] The forthright country parson from Overisel asserted that "little is heard on Christian Liberty in our Christian Reformed circles. What accounts for it? To me it seems that many consider it a dangerous doctrine to teach" (p. 21). Citing Galatians 5:1, which speaks of "the liberty wherewith Christ hath made us free," the lecturer declared that whoever remains silent about Christian liberty "belittles the work of Christ," and also "belittles the work of the Holy Spirit" (p. 23). Comparing the freedom enjoyed by him who is Christ's servant with the situation of the bondservant of the law, Kuiper grew eloquent in his description of the liberty enjoyed by the Christian:

> The servant of the law is continually beset by fear that he is going wrong. In the words of Calvin, "he will doubt whether it is lawful for him to use linen for sheets, shirts, napkins, and handkerchiefs; he will not long be secure as to hemp; and will at last have doubts as to tow." (Inst. III, 19, 7.) He hides his talent in a napkin for fear of losing it. The Christian has no such trouble. He spreads out his wings. He is active, progressive. He takes hold of things with a will. His eyes sparkle. He whistles, hums, sings. Because he lives thus, therefore he accomplishes much. His reward will be according.—The servant of law fears his fellowmen. The Christian asks exultingly: "Why is my liberty judged of another man's conscience?" (I Cor. 10:29.)—The servant of the law fears to speak. He passes through life sullenly. The Christian proclaims the great works of God freely. He can sing even in prison, as did the apostle of liberty. He resembles the bird which sings beautifully because he has the expanse of heaven for its home.—The servant of the law dreads God, the righteous Lawgiver and Judge. The Christian loves God and exclaims: "Abba, Father" (Gal. 4:6).—The servant of the law fears the punishment threatened by the law, most of all eternal damnation. Therefore he shudders at the thought of approaching death. The Christian too will be clutched in death's iron grip. Though he knows it, yet he fears not. Defiantly he sings: "Death, where is thy sting? Hell, where is thy victory?" For he knows that the sting of death is sin and that the power of sin is the law, from which he is free. (I Cor. 15:55, 56.)—The servant of the law, because he is a servant, has no claim on the Lord's possessions. The

Christian is a child: a son, a daughter. All that is the Father's is his. Earth and heaven, the heaven of heavens, are his.[4]

There is a passage in the lecture that evokes a smile. We read that "physical exercise is a necessity, but when the world makes baseball playing a profession, a business, to which men devote their lives, it goes much too far. I think the Christian should not attend professional games" (p. 21). We have to wonder whether R.B. sometimes thought of these words when he later enjoyed many a professional baseball game in Philadelphia on a free pass.

It was inevitable that such a gifted preacher could not remain long in the relative obscurity of the village of Overisel. The wish expressed by the clerk of the council[5] that the new pastor might remain for many years was not to be realized. Larger fields of service demanded his talents and his devotion to his Lord. In October of 1914 he accepted a call from the West Leonard Street Christian Reformed Church of Grand Rapids and shortly thereafter left his first charge, after a stay of two years and four months.

West Leonard Street

In accepting the call to the West Leonard Street church the R.B. Kuiper family moved into a familiar area, the area where Mrs. Kuiper had served as teacher and principal in the local Christian school. Father Klaas Kuiper preached the sermon at R.B.'s installation. The text was Paul's charge to Timothy, "Preach the Word" (II Tim. 4:2a), words which fly as a banner over all of R.B.'s years of service in Christ's kingdom. It is noteworthy that the man installed on December 6, 1914 with the admonition to "preach the Word" ringing in his ears, preached that Word in this very same church for the last time when his health began to fail toward the end of his days on earth.

His stay at West Leonard Street church was not long—just three years. But they were eventful years, years when World War I deeply affected all aspects of the nation's life. The war affected life at West Leonard Street church too. A shortage of coal in 1915-16 forced the congregation to meet for worship in the basement. Things were crowded there, and the miserable practice of teenage boys sitting apart from their parents made for problems. They sat on the outer fringes of the audience, up against the walls, and there was an occasional disturbance, much to the chagrin of the elders and the pastor.

R.B. Kuiper's reputation as a preacher continued to grow. Surviving members of the flock speak of the young pastor of those years as a "very good preacher." "You couldn't find a better one," I was told by one senior citizen at the church. The preacher's popularity took on a new dimension as invitations started to come in asking him to speak at different functions in the city and beyond. As his career unfolded his versatility as a speaker and lecturer came to be widely recognized. He spoke to many different groups at all sorts of events, always earning the warm response of his audiences with his mastery of the subject matter, his forceful delivery and his unfailing wit. He spoke to men's groups, women's groups, youth groups. He spoke to smaller local groups and to regional or national mass meetings. He spoke at graduation exercises of elementary schools, high schools, colleges and seminaries, in some instances several times at the same institution. He spoke at the dedication of school or seminary, or at anniversary affairs of such. He spoke at Bible conferences in Maine, Pennsylvania, Mississippi, Indiana and California. He spoke to organizations of business and community leaders, and to groups of employees. He spoke at many festivals for the promotion of missions. He spoke in Amsterdam and Geneva. What was the secret of R.B.'s immense popularity as a speaker? Very likely there were several reasons. A summary reason was succinctly stated in my hearing one day by Calvin K. Cummings, secretary of the League of Evangelical Students, when he said, "You can always count on R.B. to give you a good speech." Most people who heard R.B. Kuiper agreed with the judgment. On one occasion R.B. did not give a good speech; in fact, he didn't give any speech. He was scheduled to lecture in Kalamazoo but he had neglected to make the entry in his datebook. With dismay he learned of his oversight when the telephone rang in his Grand Rapids home to inform him that a church full of people was waiting for him to appear. This minor catastrophe probably happened when he was president of Calvin College.

At West Leonard Street church R.B. was regarded as being a good pastor as well as a good pulpiteer. People of the church who knew him spoke appreciatively to me of his pastoral concern. His work as pastor is reflected in a letter he wrote to the church at the time of its seventy-fifth anniversary celebration. R.B. wrote, "I baptized 89 children, 57 public confessions of faith were made. I united 31 couples in holy matrimony, and conducted 46 funerals."

The Language Question

The church had a problem that it shared with a number of congregations in the Christian Reformed Church at that time. It was the troublesome language question. Should the services continue to be held in the Dutch language that was so much part of the life of those who built the church, or should the English language take over more and more as requested by the younger members? The resolution of this problem moved slowly and required much patience, more patience probably than the high-spirited young pastor possessed. As evidenced by the language used in the publication *Christian Liberty*, R.B. could handle the English language most effectively. He fretted under the continuing burden of the language question. In his letter of congratulation cited above he said that it was not until 1917 that an occasional evening service was conducted in English. Yet a consistory minute dated September 18, 1917 reads as follows: "Decided that three worship services shall be held on Sundays during the months of November through May and two services on Sundays through the remaining six months of the year. All services shall be conducted in the Holland language."[6]

That decision can be viewed only as a setback for R.B.'s hopes for the congregation. Another related development troubled him. Some fifty families left the congregation in 1917 to form the English-speaking Twelfth Street Christian Reformed Church. The unyielding language problem no doubt had a bearing on R.B.'s acceptance of the call from the Sherman Street church late in 1917..

Chapter 6

Sherman Street

The Sherman Street Christian Reformed Church of Grand Rapids had issued a call to Reverend R.B. Kuiper in October of 1916, but the call had been declined. A year later a second call was accepted, and R.B. was installed in November of 1917 with his father participating in the service by delivering the charge to the pastor.

This was the beginning of R.B. Kuiper's happiest and most fruitful pastorate. He later wrote, "I enjoyed my Sherman Street pastorate immensely."[1] This was also his longest pastorate, coming to an end in the early fall of 1923. With the nettlesome language question behind him, the gifted young preacher could feel free to spread his wings. The crowds came to hear him. To accommodate the ever growing audiences the church almost doubled its seating capacity by installing a large balcony. Wherever R.B. Kuiper preached the crowds followed him. When he came to Sherman Street church the congregation numbered 175 families. When he left six years later there were 265 families.

The able preacher was also a faithful pastor. He was sensitive to the feelings of those he dealt with, and he was careful not to be viewed as a minister who preferred the company of the wealthier members of the flock. Mrs. Kuiper often accompanied him on his calls. The early years of the pastorate at Sherman Street church were still war years. Pastor Kuiper had a special arrangement with young men going into the service of their country and who wished to be married. He refused to accept an honorarium from such couples. Word of this was noised around and R.B. performed many marriage ceremonies of service men and their brides, also of couples not from his own congregation. The severe flu epidemic that broke out in 1918-1919 affected R.B's ministry at Sherman Street church, as, for example, in the cancellation of worship services for a period of six to eight weeks when the scourge was at its peak. Many funeral services were held, many of them small family affairs conducted on people's porches to help prevent the spread of the disease.

Lively Catechism Teacher

R.B. was also a successful catechism teacher. Classes in catechism were often looked upon by children as a drag. Not so with pastor Kuiper. His antics in class were often most entertaining. In dramatizing the story of Daniel in the lion's den he spoke from behind the spindled back of a chair, and he would also roar like a lion (something which he with his sonorous voice could do well). To depict David's exploit in killing the giant Goliath he simulated the young shepherd's action with the sling by a vigorous sweep of his arm, and then he fell prostrate on the floor. The children were delighted by the language he used. In referring to the first parents, for instance, he spoke of Mr. and Mrs. Adam. Anyone who ever heard him tell a story with his customary vividness, relish and gusto can see why the pupils enjoyed their catechism teacher. Absenteeism was not a problem in R.B. Kuiper's catechism classes. R.B.'s experience at Sherman Street church ought to remind the church that the key to successful catechism classes is not first of all the pedagogical sophistication of the materials used but rather the character and performance of the teacher.

Some interesting and funny trivia are part of the Kuiper years at Sherman Street. The preacher who had been country parson at Overisel still acted the part in the city church. R.B. maintained an ample garden and also had some chickens. He liked nothing better than to put on some slouchy old clothes and an unsightly hat in order to do his chores or his gardening. On one occasion as the preacher was leading in a worship service he was shocked to notice that he was not wearing the jacket he regularly wore on the pulpit; instead he was wearing the garment he usually wore when he fed the chickens. A feature of the landscape at Sherman Street was a city dump behind the church and parsonage. What role the dump played in R.B.'s career I do not know. His growing son loved to scrounge around in it. I can hear R.B. say, "There's one for the dump" on those occasions when he felt he had preached poorly. R.B. Kuiper had those times too.

R.B.'s excellent general education coupled with his firm commitment to the broad Calvinistic perspective on the whole of life led him to join seven other men in 1918 to issue a letter calling for the publication of a new journal "of a scholarly and artistic nature, intended especially for those who are interested in the higher things of life." The result of this effort by the eight preachers and professors was the appearance of the magazine *Religion and Culture* in May 1919. R.B. Kuiper was an associate editor along with H.J.G. Van Andel, W.H. Jellema, and J.G. Vanden Bosch. E.J. Tuuk was the editor-in-chief. Articles by R.B. appeared in many issues, not always over his signature or initials. He wrote a number of articles relating to the celebrated controversy swirling around his brother-in-law Dr. Ralph Janssen, professor of Old Testament at the Theological School. This matter is dealt with in the next chapter.

Times of Sorrow

Although R.B. Kuiper could say that he greatly enjoyed his pastorate at the Sherman Street church, this does not mean that these were years without pain. The Janssen controversy brought much distress, as the next chapter makes clear. Furthermore, there were two deaths in the family circle, deaths of loved ones who meant much to the Kuiper family. In March of 1921 father Klaas Kuiper died. He had retired in 1919 at the age of 78, and was nearly 80 years old when he passed away. The old and greatly loved father and grandfather had maintained a keen interest in church affairs to the very end. In the last letter he wrote, dated March 4, 1921, he expressed fear that the tensions over the Janssen case might lead to schism in the church. He also raised the question whether the writings of H. Hoeksema in his column in *The Banner* were sound. An earlier letter dated March 20, 1919 revealed a man with a deeply sensitive soul as he described a profound spiritual struggle he had undergone, a struggle in

which by God's grace he had overcome to arrive at a blessed
point of renewed peace and joy. The patriarch wrote his wife
and children, "Hold fast to His Word, trust His promises completely. Live tenderly and conscientiously before the Lord. Fear
nothing but sin. Be and do for one another all you can." The re-

The children: Klaudius, Kathryn Junia and Marietta.

mains of the dear husband, father and grandfather were carried to the grave by his six sons.

A sorrow that cut much more deeply came to the R.B. Kuiper home early in 1922. This searing hurt came after a period of great happiness. A third child had been born to Rev. and Mrs. R.B. Kuiper in the early autumn of 1919. Kathryn Junia was a delightful child and the entire family dearly loved her. They called her Junie. But they were to have this joy less than two and one-half years. A mastoid infection led to her death early in 1922. That event cut a deep, deep furrow in R.B. Kuiper's life. The fluent and gifted preacher stumbled in the pulpit several times after the child's death. The poignancy of the grief is revealed in a note written some four months later. The young people's society of the church invited the pastor and his wife to a banquet. The invitation drew this response: "Rev. and Mrs. Kuiper express their heartfelt thanks for your invitation to your banquet. They beg to be excused, however, from attending. Their hearts are still too heavy to take part in merriment, and they would not lessen your merriment by their presence." At the funeral of their darling child a soloist sang the hymn "Safe In The Arms Of Jesus." Thereafter R.B. could never get himself to call for or to sing this hymn.

This painful spot in R.B. Kuiper's life shows up in a tender letter he wrote to Mrs. Kuiper twelve years later. The letter reads in part as follows: "I am thankful to God that in his wise and wonderfully kind providence he led me to marry you. It is easier to put it down on paper than to say it, but I firmly believe that I could not possibly have got a better wife. My prayer is God may bless us richly for many years to come together with Marietta and Klaudius, and that in the end we may all be where our little Junia is."[2] Whenever R.B. Kuiper's preaching touched on the subject of the salvation of children who die in infancy, he always spoke with a warm and intense eloquence.

In all the years that I was part of the Kuiper family this painful memory was never spoken of in the presence of Mr. and Mrs. Kuiper. Almost half a century after the child's death Mrs. Kuiper lived for a time in our home in Florida after R.B.'s death in 1966. One day she called my wife and me to her room; there was something she wanted us to see. She opened a cardboard box and we were completely surprised and somewhat awed at

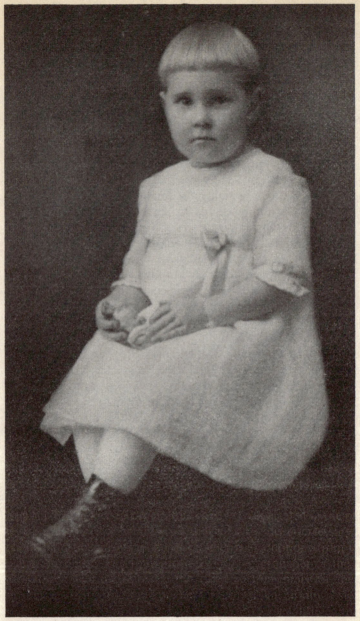

Kathryn Junia 1919-1922

what we saw. The box contained clothes that Kathryn Junia had worn. Mrs. Kuiper had treasured them all those years.

First Full-Sized Book

The happy, sad and at times troubled years of the Sherman Street church pastorate were also productive years. In that period of time R.B. baptized 195 children and three adults, and there were 136 confessions of faith. In addition R.B. produced his first full-sized book. The book, strikingly entitled *While the Bridegroom Tarries*, contains ten sermons preached at Sherman Street church after World War I on the signs of the times. "Quite a number of people nowadays," said the preacher, "are considerably excited about the signs of the times. Not a few show symptoms of extreme nervousness. Much literature written on the subject is largely responsible for this . . . The purpose of these sermons will surely be to put you on the alert, but not at all to put you on the jump."[3] Furthermore, said the preacher in characteristic style, "Our project in preaching these sermons will not be to satisfy your curiosity. If you should be looking for that, you will be disappointed. We shall try to disappoint you."[4] And he announced the primary purpose of all his pulpit work when he said, "We have no desire to preach anything but the Word."[5]

Growing unbelief in the church at large is one of the signs of the times. He hit hard at those who fail to preach and to teach the true faith. Hear the preacher as he strikes at such disloyal servants of the church.

> And now we ask: what is left of Christianity if the modern preacher is right? We answer: precisely nothing. He casts all of real Christianity before the moles and the bats. Again we ask: what comfort can be gleaned from such a gospel; what satisfaction can it give? Once more we answer: none at all. As our eyes grow dim with age, as the night of death approaches, it gives no vision of a city the gates of which are not closed by day because there is no night there. When we stand at the entrance of the valley of the dark shadows of death, peering after a dear one who just entered, it can do no better than ruthlessly rob us of all the sweet stories of heaven we learned at mother's

knee. As we entrust a beloved body to the grave, where
presently perfect darkness will reign, it offers us not the
faintest ray of light. The new religion gives us for bread a
stone, for fish a serpent, for an egg a scorpion. Its outcome is
black despair (pp. 81f.).

Missions received a powerful impulse in the events
associated with the great war, according to R.B. Kuiper. Not
every motive for missions could be applauded, but he saw the
gospel going forth worldwide at an accelerated pace. A distinction is carefully drawn between *christianizing* and *evangelizing*
the world. The latter will occur, not the former. This evangeliza-
tion must and will take place before Christ returns. Hence the
strong desire for Christ's return is a powerful stimulus for missions. "All Christians," said the preacher, "long for the coming
of their Lord. They pray very often: 'Thy kingdom come!'
Every once in a while they pray: 'Come, Lord Jesus, yea, come
quickly!' Who in *these* days does not pray that prayer every day?
There is no more fervent desire in the Christian's heart than that
Jesus may come back soon. If he is the right kind of Christian,
that desire almost consumes him."[6]
Is there hyperbole in this strong statement? Perhaps so, in
order to drive the point home. But notice the accent on the word
these before the word days. These words were spoken when the
heavy clouds of global war had not yet been fully dispersed even
though the conflict was formally ended. Even so, every Christian would do well to ponder the point in some extended and informed reflection. Perhaps Christians living in a different and
less stressful time find the present world too comfortable and attractive, as did Paul's co-worker Demas (see II Tim. 4:10).
Listen once again to the eloquent preacher.

> Ours is *the missionary age*. Tremendous, stupendous, un-
> precedented in the history of Christianity, are the missionary
> efforts put forth by the church of Christ today. Ours is also *the
> age of the church's departure from the faith*. With extreme
> rapidity is the church deteriorating spiritually. When we at-
> tempt to put these two facts together, we marvel. The thing is
> wonderful in our eyes. We see the hand of God. We exclaim:
> Behold a sign of the times. Our hearts begin to throb with joy.
> Our souls are consumed with longing. We lift our faces up-

ward. Our eyes attempt to pierce the clouds. We strain our ears
to catch the welcome sound of angels' trumpets (pp. 115f.).

While the Bridegroom Tarries is highly interesting as an in-
dex to some opinions R.B. then had, opinions which were subject to modification in later years under different conditions and
with further reflection. Who would care to be called upon to defend all the positions taken during one's lifetime? R.B. applauded the 1918 decision of the Christian Reformed Church to join
the ecumenical movement then called the Federal Council of the
Churches of Christ in America. He looked upon this action as an
instance of "standing shoulder to shoulder with the people of
God in other churches in the fight against Antichrist."[7] The
preacher declared that he expected an "actual, *literal* fulfillment" of Old Testament prophecies of Israel's return to their
ancestral land; in fact, he saw such fulfillment already "coming
true literally."[8] R.B. asked what God's purpose might be in
gathering the Jews in Palestine. He answered his own question
by saying that "God is restoring the Jewish people to Palestine
in order that presently their national conversion, foretold in the
Word, may take place. The Jewish return is God's stepping-
stone toward the incorporation of natural Israel into spiritual
Israel."[9] On another point in biblical interpretation R.B. set forth
his belief that the expression "the latter times" or "the last
days" refers to "the period just before the end of time." And he
regarded the Roman Catholic pope as "*an* Antichrist, not "*the*
Antichrist." His reasons for holding this opinion are worth
reading.[10] These views and others held by the preacher in his early thirties underwent later revision, as did the impression R.B.
was under when he observed that automobiles could "race along
the country-side at a speed of easily forty miles an hour."

Chapter 7

Controversy

The Janssen case was surely a *cause célèbre* in the Kuiper family and in the church at large. It was subject of countless conversations in the home and outside of it. Whenever family conversation would lag in those years son Klaudius would say archly, "Let's talk about the Janssen zaak for a while."

Ralph Janssen was some ten years older than his sister Marie (Mrs. R.B. Kuiper). He was an honors graduate of Hope College, school of the Reformed Church in America located in Holland, Michigan, just a few miles from the Janssen family farm home near Zeeland. He was an honor student at the University of Chicago. After graduation from Chicago he studied for four years at the University of Halle in Germany and received the Ph.D. in Philology from that school. Dr. Janssen, it is evident, was one of the best educated men in the Christian Reformed Church, and his family was proud of him. This personal aspect lent its added ingredient of pain for the Kuipers as the controversy over Janssen's views dragged on.

Janssen first served at the Theological School from 1902 to 1906 as a "lector." It seems he was viewed with some suspicion from the very beginning.[1] He was virtually unknown, his advanced education was wholly apart from the Christian Reformed Church, and he had received his doctor's degree from a university in Germany, seedbed of modern higher criticism of the Bible. Also, his advanced degree was in Philology (Linguistics), not in Theology. The semi-centennial volume of the school states that the curatorium deemed Janssen's teaching "not desirable" because of "an unmistakable leaning toward Higher Criticism." This judgment, written in 1926, may reflect

62

later developments and may thus be premature. Janssen left in 1906 to study in Scotland under the noted scholar James Orr. Then he transferred to the Free University of Amsterdam, from which he was graduated with high honors as a Doctorandus in Theology. After some years of teaching in Illinois, another appointment came in 1914 to teach at the Theological School.[2] He was chosen from a trio composed of Dr. W. Bode, Dr. R. Janssen and Dr. S. Volbeda. Volbeda was elected to replace Rev. G.D. De Jong.[3] It appears that Janssen was appointed at this time in the confidence that his study under Bavinck and Kuyper in Amsterdam had cleared up whatever questions that had emerged in his previous tenure.

The Gathering Storm

But Professor Janssen was not home clear. After just a few years the storm broke over his head. On the basis of a persistent flow of reports coming to them from students, Dr. Janssen's four colleagues came to the Board of Trustees in June of 1919 to ask for an investigation of the teaching of their fellow instructor. The response of the Board was a rebuke to the four professors for not having conferred with Dr. Janssen before coming to the ruling body of the school. The four professors were not satisfied and announced they would appeal to the next session of the synod. This spurred the Board to take up the matter again and to undertake a "thorough" investigation. The result was a three-point decision in which the Board expressed its satisfaction with Janssen's view of the inspiration of Scripture, declared that the problems would disappear through brotherly discussions, and called upon Dr. Janssen so to teach that misunderstandings would not arise.

The four professors felt their concerns were not set aside and they appealed to the Synod of 1920. That body decided to go through all the documents in the case and to hear all the principal figures involved. The four professors spoke in turn and then Dr. Janssen held the floor for the larger part of an afternoon session and also for a time the next morning. The upshot was to uphold the decision of the Board of Trustees, with one exception: the synod set aside the Board's determination that the four professors should have conferred with Janssen prior to bringing their concern to the governing body. No grounds are given for this judgment of the synod,[4] a judgment that seems puzzling in view of Matthew 7:12, 18:15ff., I Corinthians 14:40. A more gracious approach to a presumably erring brother in Christ might have forestalled some of the rancor and sharp rhetoric that appeared as the controversy progressed.[5]

The Role of Rev. H. Hoeksema

Once Dr. Janssen's teaching had been discussed at synod the door was opened for the introduction of the case to the wider church public. The door was opened especially by Rev. Herman Hoeksema, pastor of the Eastern Avenue Christian Reformed Church in Grand Rapids. He did this by means of his column in the church publication *The Banner*. In this column, labelled *Our Faith*, Hoeksema asserted his disagreement with the decision of the synod, and then proceeded to deal with the issues in the case. He made the church at large aware of the existence of student notes on Janssen's class lectures as he quoted from these notes. The winds of controversy began to blow ever harder. Different publications, some previously existing, some new ones, joined in the battle on either side. A number of pamphlets appeared, notably Janssen's "The Crisis in the Christian Reformed Church" and a response entitled "What the Janssen Case Is All About."[6] The latter was put out over the names of the four colleagues of Janssen and four pastors. The pastors were H. Danhof, Y.P. De Jong, H. Hoeksema and H.J. Kuiper, all of Grand Rapids.

Dr. Janssen's handling of the Old Testament Scriptures was at the heart of the problem. He steadfastly avowed his devotion to the church's teaching on the authority and infallibility of the Bible. But his critics insisted this avowal was made questionable by his views on the authorship and makeup of the first five books of the Bible, his teaching regarding other books such as Job and the Song of Solomon, and his explanation of the miracles of the Old Testament. It was further alleged that Janssen's teaching stressed the human and historical-developmental factors in biblical history so much that the all-important and governing divine factor was obscured. He was charged with dealing with the books of the Bible, not as an organism of divine revelation, but as separate documents to be examined by the methods of scientific research and criticism. In this connection his critics said that his teaching made very little use of New Testament revelation in his understanding of Old Testament data.[7]

The critics based their case on student notes on Janssen's class lectures. This fact was occasion for much dispute. Was it proper to use these student notes to make a case against the teacher? Janssen insisted that the student notes did not accurately reflect his own views. Two former students who had edited their own notes and had allowed them to be mimeographed let it be known that their notes were individual notes, not compilations of notes taken by several students, and that some selection, adjustment and rewriting was done prior to their production in mimeographed form. Hence, the two students declared, Dr. Janssen should not be held accountable for the contents of the notes.[8] The two students were H. Schultze, later professor at Calvin Seminary and president of Calvin College, and F.H. Wezeman, himself in 1936-37 the central figure in a controversy over his teaching of Bible at the Chicago Christian High School.

The problem that arose with respect to the use of these student notes was that no other materials were available to those examining Janssen's teaching. Even when specifically asked for, no materials were furnished by Dr. Janssen. R.B. Kuiper has been quoted as saying that his brother-in-law had no set of notes from which he "dictated" to his classes.[9] This was a delicate point, and the objection by the professor and his supporters to the use made of these notes in the controversy is wholly understandable. Such notes surely could not be understood to articulate in precise detail what the teacher said in the classroom at any particular point. On the other hand, such notes could be viewed as a fairly accurate representation of what the teaching conveyed to the students, even though these notes had undergone some editing by the students taking them. What the notes contained was what the students absorbed from the instruction given. After all, the church would have to be concerned with the end product of the teaching, namely, that which

was in the minds of those who received the instruction, even
though the exact language involved in that instruction could not
be traced. When the kind of evidence furnished by the student
notes was joined with the testimonies of students who were per-
plexed by the professor's teaching and with reports of the appearance of the disputed views in examinations of candidates for the
ministry, then the "sufficient grounds of suspicion" that the Christian Reformed Church officially speaks of were clearly present.[11]

The Church Stirred

Widespread distribution of the mimeographed student
notes together with H. Hoeksema's punchy writing in his column in *The Banner* stirred the church at large to act. Two-thirds
of the church classes called upon the Board of Trustees to make
a thorough investigation of Janssen's teaching. In June 1921 the
Board acceded, appointed an investigative committee, and gave
Dr. Janssen a year's vacation with pay. In a critical editorial in
Religion and Culture (Aug. 1921) R.B. Kuiper used the term
suspension for that which the Board euphemistically called a
"vacation with pay." This punitive action, said Kuiper, was
taken without an official charge against the professor and after
he had been exonerated twice by the Board and once by synod.
This was "no small injustice" according to R.B.

Janssen refused to cooperate with the investigating committee, would not give them materials they asked for, and would
not appear before them. His strongest objection to the committee was that it had among its members men whose views were
unReformed. He had reference especially to H. Danhof and H.
Hoeksema, men who three years later (that is, in 1924) left the
Christian Reformed Church over the issue of Common Grace.
On this point we have R.B. Kuiper's opinion in the following
words: "How it (the curatorium) blundered when it placed two
men on the committee whose doctrinal soundness was under
suspicion! Manifestly that should never have been done. Men
who flatly denied the Reformed doctrine of common grace were
unfit to pass judgment on the Reformed character of Janssen's
teachings, the more so since he made so very much of this particular truth."[11]

The work of the investigating committee resulted in a split report. A majority of four members brought a sharply critical report, a minority of three a less critical one. But both reports agreed that Janssen's kind of teaching had no place at the Theological School. After both reports were heard by the Board in March of 1922, a motion to invite Dr. Janssen to defend himself was defeated by a vote of 13-11,[12] an unfortunate action prompted largely, no doubt, by the professor's refusal to cooperate with the committee. This action elicited several protests, one by nine members of the Board. A protest was also registered by the consistory of the Sherman Street church.

Orange City in northwestern Iowa was the setting for the historic meeting of the synod which deposed Dr. Janssen. The gathering had before it the two reports of the investigative committee together with a large number of overtures in the matter as well as protests against the failure of the previous synod to repudiate Janssen's teaching. The synod's advisory committee in the matter invited Dr. Janssen to appear before it so that he might correct from his own materials any items that the investigative committee had taken from the student notes. Janssen appeared before the advisory committee, but declined to make any comment beyond the reading of a prepared statement in which he expressed his judgment that it was impossible for him to receive a "fair trial" before the synod under the prevailing circumstances.

Janssen Deposed

The advisory committee also recommended that the professor be given opportunity to defend himself on the floor of synod. This was a critical point in the movement of the Janssen case at synod. R.B. Kuiper strongly advised his brother-in-law to speak in his own defense. "If you don't do so," R.B. told him, "you may as well take the next train out of here." Janssen persisted in his refusal to speak. He maintained that there were those at synod who were prosecutors as well as judges, people who had made up their minds about him, people who had spoken or written publicly against him. He said he would be glad to discuss all the points in dispute, but only if his objections to the stacked makeup of synod and the violations of good order were acknowledged.[13] Dr. Janssen was deposed. The intensity of feeling present at the time was demonstrated by the quotation of the words of Psalm 139:21-22 just prior to the vote on the motion to depose—"Do not I hate them, Lord, that hate thee? . . . I hate them with a perfect hatred."[14]

Obviously such a boiling issue with its long history could not die at once after the action of the Synod of 1922. Supporters of Dr. Janssen and other sympathizers launched a National Movement in the Janssen Case.[15] Meetings were held in Grand Rapids and Chicago in September of 1922. The notebooks containing the minutes of these two meetings have record of no other formal gatherings of the National Movement. The project envisioned a rather ambitious program, including plans to underwrite Janssen's living costs at $250 per month, to bring protest against the action of the synod, to put out a publication to promote their views, and to undertake a study of the subject of Common Grace. The desirability of establishing a new theological school free from church control was debated but not acted on. R.B. Kuiper was appointed to a committee to draw up a protest. It seems that this National Movement did not accomplish a great deal. Participants were scattered from Grand Rapids to Chicago to central Iowa, and monies to cover the monthly payments to Dr. Janssen and other costs were not easily raised. The group probably made a capital mistake in choosing B.K. Kuiper as its secretary. Able, yes, even brilliant writer and thinker he was, but he was not the man to look after the nuts and bolts of the project's ongoing administration and promotion.[16]

Assessment

At this point a probing question has to be asked. Were all of Janssen's sympathizers convinced that his teaching was free from the undesirable features alleged against it? There were strong objections to glaring procedural faults that had marred the handling of the Janssen matter from the beginning, faults which in the eyes of the sympathizers constituted a grave injustice to the learned professor. But in the substantive issue were all convinced of the full correctness of his teaching? A revealing sentence from the pen of none other than R.B. Kuiper sheds light on this question. Appealing for "doctrinal balance" in theology, R.B. illustrates his point by saying, "Let us be careful not to emphasize the supernatural origin of the Bible so strongly that our view of inspiration becomes mechanical, but, on the other hand, let us also beware, as of poison, of the leaven of those who stress the human element in Scripture at the expense of the divine."[17] One can hardly fail to recognize the second strongly worded part of that quotation as an unmistakable reference to what was a major element in the case against Dr. Janssen. In a private coversation I had with R.B. some years later after he had become my father-in-law, he answered a question I had put to him in the matter by saying that in his judgment Janssen's teaching had not been free from the taint of Higher Criticism.

The Janssen case reappeared at the Synod of 1924. A number of protests against the action of the previous synod had to be dealt with, but there was no protest at synod brought by the committee named for that purpose by the National Move-. ment in the Janssen Case. The Synod of 1924, which met for three weeks at Kalamazoo, Michigan, is best known for its three-point affirmation of the doctrine of Common Grace. This pronouncement shortly led to the departure of Rev. H. Hoeksema, Rev. H. Danhof and others from the Christian Reformed Church in order to form a new denomination called the Protestant Reformed Church. But the sticky Common Grace issue apparently did not take as much of the synod's time as did the protests having to do with Janssen's deposition. Seventy-five pages of the official *Acts* of the 1924 Synod are devoted to the handling of these protests, whereas less than half that number of pages are devoted to the Common Grace question. The delegates in 1924 resolutely supported the action of the Synod of 1922 regarding Dr. Janssen. Having some bearing on this fact was another curious twist in the history of the Janssen case. The two ministers who wrote the advisory committee's report at the Synod of 1922 were the same men to head the advisory committee dealing with the protests at the Synod of 1924.[18] These two able men were D.H. Kromminga and H.J. Kuiper, men who subsequently would serve the Christian Reformed Church in positions of leadership, the former as professor at Calvin

Seminary and the latter as editor of *The Banner* for many years. H.J. Kuiper and R.B. Kuiper were not related.

Thus ended the Janssen case with its long and agonizing history. It brought much heartache to the learned professor and his family. To the church it brought years of struggle, struggle which at times seemed to threaten schism. To R.B. Kuiper it was a painfully educative experience, an experience which would stand him in good stead when some years later he would stand on the front lines of the battle for orthodox Christianity.[19] A church historian's comment on the significance of the case is worth quoting. Calling the Janssen case "the first measurable indication of the impact of liberalism" upon the church, J.H. Kromminga wrote, "It became apparent that the Christian Reformed Church was not willing to have the slightest doubt cast upon the infallibility of the Bible."[20]

Chapter 8

Reformed Church in America

No one could have predicted how the satisfying pastorate at Sherman Street church would come to an end. It may as well be said that any such predictions were pointless in R.B.'s case. He was always his own man and tailored his actions to his own thinking. What others might think of his actions had little to do with his decisions. It was not easy for him to leave Sherman Street church. Three years after leaving he spoke of the "inward pain" he suffered when he felt "compelled" to sever this close bond. In the fall of 1923 he accepted a call to become pastor in another denomination, one against which he admitted he had been "somewhat prejudiced." He became pastor of the Second Reformed Church of Kalamazoo, Michigan. One facet of this event was consistent with a pattern R.B. never departed from. The new pastorate was in the state of Michigan, where all the churches he served were located.

Light is thrown on this surprising move by R.B. himself in a book he wrote in 1926. In the preface to *As To Being Reformed* he wrote as follows: "When I left the Christian Reformed Church, I was convinced that, in view of certain conditions which then prevailed in that denomination, I could do more for the Kingdom in the Reformed Church in America." The "certain conditions" in the Christian Reformed Church to which R.B. alluded had to do with the doctrinal controversies that had been so prominent in the previous decade. To some people it seemed that the people in the Christian Reformed Church were always fighting. R.B. related an incident in which some one spoke to him at a time when he was considering a call from a Christian Reformed congregation. "You don't want to go back

71

there, " R.B. was told; "they are always fighting." R.B.'s pointed reply was, "There are churches that badly need a good fight."[1]

The conditions in the Christian Reformed church that led to Kuiper's departure in 1923 were not in his eyes the doctrinal controversies as such. These controversies were a sign of health; they demonstrated that the Christian Reformed Church took doctrine seriously. "While the Christian Reformed Church was torn by conflict," R.B. wrote, "many other churches seemed to be enjoying enviable peace. But let us not be deceived by the appearance of things. There is a peace which is no peace. Peace obtained at the expense of truth is not worthy of its name. There are churches that ascribe their apparent peace to doctrinal tolerance, while as a matter of fact they are guilty of doctrinal indifference, the wages of which are death. Cemeteries too are peaceful places . . . Let no member of the Christian Reformed Church be ashamed of his membership in a denomination that regards purity of doctrine worth fighting for. It is reason for just pride."[2]

Why He Went

R.B. Kuiper's problems with the Christian Reformed Church at the time related not to the *what* of these controversies, but to their *how*, to the manner in which they were carried on. And here R.B. cited two serious shortcomings, namely, the lack of justice or fairness, and the lack of love toward those suspected of erring. It is evident and understandable that R.B. was especially concerned with such shortcomings as they showed up in the handling of the Janssen case. He had been greatly troubled by these failures in proper procedure. He had been especially distressed at the prominent role played by Rev. H. Hoeksema and Rev. H. Danhof in the process that led finally to Janssen's deposition, since these men had publicly declared their rejection of an element of Reformed doctrine that was important to R.B. Kuiper.

The question must be asked, was R.B.'s keen dissatisfaction with the way the Janssen case had been handled reason enough for him to end a happy pastorate, leave the denomination and join himself to one which, by his own word, did not stand high in his esteem? The situation appears to have been somewhat more complex. The Janssen case had put R.B. in a difficult position. His personal ties to Ralph Janssen had exacerbated his feelings of outrage at faults in the handling of the case. In this connection the emotional ties of Mrs. Kuiper to her highly regarded brother must not be overlooked. She, a strong-minded woman, suffered unmitigated pain at the treatment he received. But then there was the substantive issue. In the previous chapter we have noted that R.B. was not convinced that Janssen was wholly sound in his views. R.B. had spent a year at Princeton Seminary. There he had studied under scholars who were thoroughly conversant with Higher Criticism of the Bible and who had championed the cause against these destructive views. The name of Princeton's Robert Dick Wilson was a household word among informed clergy as a world-renowned leader in the battle against Higher Criticism. So R.B. knew full well that the views reflected in the student notes taken under Janssen's instruction were unacceptable in a seminary true to its Reformed confession. No other estimate of his position on the substantive issue in the Janssen case seems tenable.

This tension between R.B.'s personal feelings regarding the treatment Janssen had received and his judgment of the correctness of the professor's views made for an intense internal struggle. Something had to happen to relieve the situation. He needed some fresh air. The opportunity to break out of his oppressive dilemma came when the Second Reformed Church of Kalamazoo invited him to preach in the spring of 1923. He declined the invitation. The invitation came again in the following summer. He accepted and preached one of his favorite sermons. The theme of the sermon was "What Is Truth?", the words of Pilate taken from John 18:38. He developed the subject under four heads: (1) God is truth; (2) Christ is truth; (3) the Bible is truth; (4) the Reformed interpretation of the Bible is truth. The sermon got an impressive response; R.B. was thrilled at what he saw. He sensed that the people were hungry for that kind of preaching. The church called him in September. As he was considering the call the consistory of the church, entirely of its own accord, assured him that he was being called precisely because they very much wanted the kind of preaching his sermon had demonstrated. R.B. wrote, "I felt it my sacred duty with the aid of God's grace to help satisfy this hunger and quench this thirst."[3]

Accident in Chicago

The start of the ministry in Kalamazoo was complicated by a grievous turn of events. Before settling down to the new routine in Kalamazoo the Kuipers decided to make a brief visit to Uncle John Kuiper and family in Roseland, Chicago. While they were there on the way to the Field museum, a man speeding along in his new automobile smashed broadside into Uncle John's seven-passenger touring car. Mrs. Kuiper was sitting on the side that was hit and sustained a badly damaged pelvis. The injury required several weeks of hospitalization in Chicago, and left her with a condition which, when complicated by arthritis, made walking difficult in her later years. This unfortunate occurrence delayed R.B.'s entrance upon his duties at Second Reformed Church, and led to a schedule that included many trips to Chicago. Mrs. Kuiper and children remained there until the snow began to fall. Marietta and Klaudius enjoyed their stay in Roseland. They attended the local Christian school and had a great time with their four cousins, at whose home they stayed.

R.B. expressed warm appreciation for the congregation in Kalamazoo. He cited its warm friendliness, its avid interest in missions, its fine response to Reformed preaching, also catechismal preaching. He said he never had a church where more was said and done to encourage him in his work. And when he left after two short years he made it a point to make clear that his departure was not due to any dissatisfaction he found with the congregation.

The sojourn in the Reformed Church in America was unexpectedly short for reasons that had to do with views and practices prevalent in the denomination generally. This does not mean that R.B. was without appreciation for certain commendable features he saw in the Reformed Church in America. He spoke favorably, for instance, of the denomination's theological school in Holland, Michigan, the Western Theological Seminary. And he expressed satisfaction with the

Reformed quality of articles appearing regularly in the publication *The Leader* from the pen of its "very able editor," Dr. J.E. Kuizenga. But these and other favorable factors were offset by several things that deeply troubled Kuiper, such as the neglect of distinctively Reformed teachings like the covenant of grace and predestination, carelessness in receiving into church membership people who held un-Reformed beliefs, and the openly questioning attitude of many ministers toward the church's Reformed confessions. Especially one significant action persuaded R.B. of the denomination's doctrinal laxity. This was the appointment by synodical decision of Dr. Edward S. Worcester to the chair of Systematic Theology at New Brunswick Theological Seminary in New Jersey. Dr. Worcester was an urbane gentleman, pastor of a Congregational church in Vermont. There was ample evidence available to all interested parties of Worcester's questionable views. Kuiper quoted Worcester as calling the doctrine of original sin "a bit of fanciful and allegorizing theology of the Rabbinic period of Judaism and similar schools in Christianity, which is worse than meaningless today."[4] Worcester objected to the word "wholly" in the phrase "wholly incapable of doing any good" in the Heidelberg Catechism's description of unsaved man. There were those who opposed the election of Dr. Worcester, and it took several ballots before the required three-fourths majority was achieved. What disturbed R.B. was the fact that the final ballot was almost unanimous. R.B. wrote, "The case of Dr. Worcester convinced me that I could not possibly feel at home in the Reformed Church in America."[5]

The Common Grace Synod

An important event occurring in the two years of the Kalamazoo pastorate was the meeting of the synod of the Christian Reformed Church in 1924. The synod, we have indicated previously, dealt with the doctrine of Common Grace and set forth this doctrine in a three-point statement. We may be sure that R.B. was a very close observer at this gathering in his own city. The doctrine of Common Grace was of utmost importance to R.B. Kuiper. He made clear that if the Synod of 1924 had taken "a less firm stand" in the matter, he would not have been "altogether so ready to return" to the Christian Reformed Church."[6] R.B. made a lucid statement of the significance of this doctrine in a paper he read at a conference of Reformed Church leaders in the spring of 1924, a paper which was published in full in *The Leader* and reproduced in his book *As To Being Reformed*. "This truth," said R.B., "keeps the Calvinist from the weakness of Fundamentalism, and at once arms him for the conflict with Modernism."[7] Fundamentalism, carrying in it "a pronounced strain of Anabaptism," fails to do justice to the riches of human life and culture. Modernism, on the other hand, loses itself in unregenerate human life because it fails to reckon with the supernatural on the one hand and with the total depravity of man on the other. Following is an example of R.B.'s strong thinking on the subject.

> The burning question is: just how good or how bad is man? The doctrine of common grace gives a definite answer to that question. It tells us that natural, unregenerated, man is totally depraved and consequently incapable of doing any good whatsoever of himself. Undeniable fact is, however, that he does a great deal of good. Just think of the civic virtues and the noble morality which often adorn him. This good, says our doctrine, is the fruit of the working of God's common grace in him.

> But now observe to what erroneous views of man the denial of common grace must needs lead. If we discard common grace, we are driven inevitably to one of two conclusions: either man is not totally depraved, he can do good of himself; or the good which he does is not really good at all: his virtues are faults; his noble accomplishments are works of the devil; his patriotism, marital fidelity, filial piety, love for his children, common honesty are all of them glittering sins. In the doctrine of man the denial of common grace leads to rankest Modernism or blackest misanthropy.

> If the church would escape being perched on either horn of this dilemma, it must cling tooth and nail to the truth of common grace.[8]

The Kalamazoo years left some indelible impressions on the children. Marietta often spoke with pleasure of times when she would meet her father after school and they together went to the local drugstore to enjoy an ice cream soda. Klaudius' memory was a bit different. He recalled that something seemed to be

Pastor R.B. Kuiper at age 38.

bothering his father at the time. He became annoyed with his son over trivial matters. R.B.'s style of life and work was to give everything he had to a cause he fully believed in. Such wholehearted devotion to his work was difficult for R.B. in a denomination in which he was beginning to feel that he was a stranger. This growing sense of estrangement with its attendant inner stress may have surfaced in his dealings with his son. But all the while he was laying up valuable reserves of experience that would serve him well in the most productive time of his life still lying ahead of him by a few years.

Chapter 9

The Downtown Church

In the autumn of 1925 R.B. Kuiper returned to the Christian Reformed Church. He took a call to the LaGrave Avenue Christian Reformed Church of Grand Rapids. This was the fifth call he received from Christian Reformed churches in the time he had been at Second Reformed. So the Christian Reformed Church had not forgotten its gifted son. Two of the calls came from churches in northwest Iowa and the others were from churches in Grand Rapids. One of the earlier calls had stipulated three worship services per Sunday, two of them in the Dutch language and the third in English. Getting involved in the language question again did not appeal to R.B. Furthermore, he felt, as he later also taught his students at Westminster Seminary, that a minister cannot produce three good sermons per week on a regular basis. The five calls did not differ very much in the salary offered. The LaGrave Avenue call had one factor that must have seemed very attractive. It offered "free use of an automobile." But questions of salary and added perquisites were not of high importance to R.B. This he plainly stated at a time when I was considering a call. The more important considerations had to do, he said, with questions such as where one can render the greater service, where one thinks he can be the most effective, and where the greatest need is.

Whatever the reasons, R.B. Kuiper was ready to end his self-imposed exile from the Christian Reformed Church. The wounds of the Janssen case had healed somewhat, the Christian Reformed Church had taken a firm stand on the matter of common grace, and R.B. had learned firsthand that the Reformed Church in America was not his home. Furthermore, LaGrave

79

Avenue church offered a special kind of challenge, one which appealed to R.B.'s adventurous spirit with its freedom from the bindings of tradition or group pressure. LaGrave Avenue church was not the typical Christian Reformed church. For one thing the church had a choir, had had this feature for some time. A spokesman for the church wrote that "LaGrave had to endure much criticism on this account."[1] The church had a reputation for being progressive; some people called LaGrave liberal or worldly, labels the church hardly deserved. It was the downtown church. It counted among its members a good many who were prominent in the city's professional and business circles.

Shortly after R.B. Kuiper came to LaGrave Avenue church there was a small gathering at the parsonage on a Sunday evening. Among the invited guests was the church's most recent pastor, Rev. Wm. Stuart. He had been a colleague of R.B.'s father in Roseland, and had just begun a productive period of service as teacher of Bible at the Grand Rapids Christian High School. Naturally the talk centered on the congregation the one had just pastored for ten years and that R.B. had just begun to serve. The pastors discussed the spiritual condition of the church and what was needed to build up the body of Christ in that place. Stuart ended the discussion in his typically direct and crisp fashion as he said to his successor, "I'm sure you can handle it."

Conscientious pastor that he was and always bent on building up the church of Christ, R.B. tackled the job. He always sought to tailor his sermonizing to what he perceived to be the needs of the congregation, and he did not shrink from preaching what he genuinely felt had to be preached. So before long he launched into a series of sermons on the general subject of the wages of sin and the wonder of God's grace. He poured out his soul in eloquent exposition of God's wondrous grace (his favorite theme), and he pulled no punches as he described the inevitable lot of those who did not repent of their sins. He did not hesitate to speak again and again of the terribleness of hell. A member told him she did not want to hear any more about hell. But R.B. did what he believed he had to do. To do otherwise would be to play games with the eternal destiny of people's souls. It was while he was at LaGrave Avenue church that he wrote as follows about the minister's conviction that he is called by God, "This conviction, safeguarding him against the fatal error of seeking to please men rather than God, will make of him a veritable hero who in reckless self-abandonment proclaims the full truth regardless of consequences.''

His Second Book

These words came from R.B.'s second book *As To Being Reformed* (page 150), which appeared less than a year after he came to LaGrave Avenue church. The preface bore the date June 18, 1926, which marked the fifteenth anniversary of the marriage of Rev. and Mrs. R.B. Kuiper. The book has already been quoted a number of times in connection with the Janssen case and the pastorate at Kalamazoo. However, as R.B. pointed out, the book is not mainly about those episodes in his life. The book's principal subject was "CALVINISM, primarily in its theological aspect." Two perceptions growing out of the Kalamazoo experience prompted him to write the book, namely, "The imminent peril in which we American Calvinists are of losing our precious Reformed heritage, and the supreme importance of our holding it fast."[2]

The book was widely read. I recall that we had the book in our home when I was a boy living in Iowa. It was this book that gave me my first awareness of the person named R.B. Kuiper. Forty years later John Vander Ploeg, editor of *The Banner*, wrote this, "For most of us, few books stand out long in our memories, but the mark left upon me by reading R.B.'s *As To Being Reformed* many years ago has not yet been forgotten."[3] The book's earthy and robust language could not fail to leave its mark. In warning against worldliness R.B. wrote, "Our parents were comparatively poor. Some of us are rich, many more are well-to-do. And almost all of us can afford to be worldly. That is, we think we can. Fools that we are." In expressing his keen displeasure with modernism R.B. said bluntly, "Modernism is perfectly despicable . . . Modernism is damnable." He spoke of the intense discussions of doctrine that he had heard as ministers sometimes met in his father's house. These discussions revealed sharp differences of opinion among the discussants, R.B. wrote, "But they were no heresy-hunters. Most of them had hearts as big as hams."

How blessed the church was to receive guidance and inspiration from writings like the chapters in this book. We discern in these chapters many of the positions and affirmations that are the insignia of this man's ministry and legacy. The chapter on "Modernism and Fundamentalism" made crystal clear that the church's home is with neither of these, although the Calvinist feels a closer kinship to the latter than to the former. The chapter on "Christianity and Calvinism" enunciated a conviction that flies as a banner over all of R.B. Kuiper's work and words, namely, that "Calvinism is the most nearly perfect interpretation of Christianity. In final analysis, Calvinism and Christianity are practically synonymous. It follows that he who departs from Calvinism is taking a step away from Christianity."[4] Any Christian living today can find rich nourishment in the chapters on "The Doctrine of Absolute Predestination," "The Importance of the Doctrine of Common Grace for the Church Today," "The Christian and the World," "Reformed Preaching," and "Christian Education." R.B. never forgot as he wrote that he was a pastor. He did not write to satisfy the academic's desire for some novel insight or the pleasure of the literati in discovering some exciting new use of words. He wrote to instruct the church member in the riches of the faith, to lay upon his people the high responsibility of giving their children a thorough Christian schooling, and to give them clear guidance as they traveled in and through the world with its slippery paths.

His Third Book

Another book came from R.B.'s pen in his LaGrave Avenue years. Like the previous volumes, it bore a title of four words, *Not of the World*. It was published in 1929. As indicated in the preface the title came from the words of Christ in his intercessory prayer, John 17:16. The volume contains eight sermons from the LaGrave Avenue pulpit. Wm. B. Eerdmans, founder of the Wm. B. Eerdmans Publishing Company and a member of the congregation, suggested that the sermons be taken down stenographically as delivered. This was done and very little editing followed, so that here we have vintage R.B. Kuiper, the pulpiteer.

Refreshing, unconventional—by such words R.B.'s way of saying things is well described. This is borne out by the chapter headings of this book, headings that invite one urgently to read what the preacher had to say. The chapter headings also indicate that R.B. was seeking to give a balanced, thoroughly biblical presentation of the complex question of the Christian's relation to the world. These arresting headings were as follows:

MINGLING WITH THE WORLD—A Good Mixer (I Cor. 5:9,10)
DIFFERING FROM THE WORLD—A True Aristocrat (Romans 12:2)
ENJOYING THE WORLD—A Healthy Human (I Cor. 7:13)
OVERCOMING THE WORLD—A Victorious Soldier (I John 5:4)
HATED BY THE WORLD—A Happy Martyr (John 16:33)
TRAVELING THROUGH THE WORLD—A Yearning Pilgrim (Heb. 11:13)
OWNING THE WORLD—A Multi-Millionaire (I Cor. 3:22,23)
EVANGELIZING THE WORLD—An Ardent Missionary (Mark 16:15)

The author stressed the necessity of taking the message of the book as a whole in order to get the proper balanced perspective. A sermon like "Enjoying the World" should not, for instance, be considered apart from the counterbalancing thrust of the other sermons. The sermons reveal the orderliness that marked R.B. Kuiper's thought processes. They also demonstrate his capacity to develop a text from Scripture so as to draw from it the full measure of its wealth and applicability to the lives of those sitting in the pews. In addition they reveal a preacher who had exceptional gifts of illustration by way of story or poem or some intriguing, interesting or amusing facet of life.

These eight sermons encouraged his listeners (and readers) to participate actively in the life that God has given His children to live in the wonderful world of which He is Creator, Ruler and Savior. Such participation cannot avoid all danger. Said the preacher, "In attempting to avoid every possible danger, we would be driven to the absurd position of the mother who forbade her children to go near water until they had learned to swim. In view of the impossibility of getting away from all danger and the absurdity of trying to do it, the apostle says (in the text of the sermon, I Cor. 5:9,10) that the only way to avoid all contact with the world is to get out of it. In order to preclude the possibility of contamination by the world, we would have to jump off the globe. Try it, and see how far you get."[5]

Indeed, to be a Christian is to be up and doing in the world, a world in which by common grace the Christian has much in common with the worldling. But, there is the other side of the coin. The Christian and the worldling, both in the world, live totally different lives. Said the preacher,

> There is between them an absolute antithesis.
> The Christian is spiritually alive; the worldling is dead in sins and trespasses. The Christian loves God; the worldling hates him. And how different is their evaluation of things! What you and I consider very valuable the world thinks of no account at all, and what the world thinks very valuable you and I hold of little account. The things which are seen are temporal and of little value to us, but not so to the world. The things which are not seen are eternal and of infinite value to us, but the world thinks nothing of them.
> It follows that, when the child of the world and the child of God do the same thing, they yet do different things. That is a paradox, but it is true.[6]

As simple but telling illustration R.B. used the daily, universal practice of eating. While both may eat the same thing, they do it very differently. The Christian does it to the glory of God—moderately, with thanksgiving, with intent to be strengthened for service to God and neighbor. The worldling does it to please himself, to satisfy his visceral cravings, to sustain physical existence.

"Landmarks and Sandmarks"

As indicated earlier R.B. was much in demand as a lecturer as well as a preacher. One lecture that drew considerable attention he named "Landmarks and Sandmarks." It is not clear just when he first delivered this lecture. It was most likely in his years as a Grand Rapids pastor, probably in the time he was at the LaGrave Avenue church. The discourse, with its cue taken from Proverbs 22:28 ("Remove not the ancient landmark . . ."), distinguished between God-prescribed traditions (landmarks) and man-made traditions (sandmarks). His main point was that only the former should bind the conscience of the Christian, although the practices he called sandmarks could be of such value that to discard them would constitute a significant loss. A landmark, according to R.B., would be the regular preaching of the Word or the celebration of the Lord's Supper. A sandmark so designated by R.B. was the practice of regular catechism preaching; another was one's choice of time when to hold daily devotions.

The lecture deserves comment for several reasons. First of all it illustrated R.B.'s striking use of alliteration, a device that not only drew the hearer's attention but also helped to make his point stick in their minds. Secondly, the speech demonstrated that R.B. had clear ideas as to what he thought was truly important and basic for the Christian's life and walk. He was never a man given to majoring in minors. In the third place the lecture showed that R.B. was not afraid to tackle touchy subjects. He later indicated that he received considerable criticism from different quarters, especially on the "sandmarks" section of the speech. Some critics felt that he attached too much importance to some of his "sandmarks," while other thought he gave them too little standing.[7]

In the four years that R.B. Kuiper was at LaGrave Avenue church the membership grew from 200 to 265 families. That his work was greatly appreciated was evident from a commentary on his pastorate appearing in a booklet prepared in connection with the fortieth anniversary banquet of the church held in February of 1927. Here we read the following: "During the year and one half that our present pastor, the Rev. R.B. Kuiper, is with us, much prosperity may already be observed. The membership has enlarged to two hundred thirty-five families; our contribution to the salary of our missionary pastor has been increased to $2,500.00; the debt incurred with the recent improvements of the church auditorium has been practically wiped out. That the pastor is prized can easily be observed from the attendance at the church services."[8]

Three Synodical Study Committees

Upon his return to the Christian Reformed Church R.B.'s gifts were soon put to use in service of the denomination. The Synod of 1926 placed R.B. on a committee to study the amusement problem. In 1928 he was placed on three different synodical study committees. One of those had to do with the principle of "free study" by those seeking admission to the ministry in the Christian Reformed Church.[9] Another committee to which R.B. was appointed was mandated to study the matter of introducing more hymns into the worship services. The result of this committee's work was the appearance of the *Psalter Hymnal* in 1934. Prior to that date the Christian Reformed Church had sung metrical renderings of the Psalms almost exclusively in its services, singing these from the church's praisebook *The Psalter*. This volume contained only three hymns, although the Church Order had up to 1932 mentioned nine hymns approved for public worship. The revision in 1932 of Article 69 of the Church Order then in force made way for the introduction of a large number of additional hymns by way of the *Psalter Hymnal*.

The Committee on Worldly Amusements, with R.B. as member, brought an extensive report to the Synod of 1928. This report and the action on it became a celebrated matter in the life of the Christian Reformed Church. R.B. always regretted the fact that among the church people generally the opinion prevailed that the Christian Reformed Church, by the action of the Synod of 1928, singled out and condemned theater-attendance, card-playing and dancing as the three outstanding forms of worldly amusement, and that this was the whole meaning of the synodical action of 1928. He felt this way for two reasons. In the first place he felt this popular notion did discredit to the report of the study committee and to the action of synod. The report and the decision of synod set forth a splendid statement of principles by which "all our amusements, not only theater-attendance, dancing and card-playing, should be judged."[10] In the second place this popular notion falls into the trap of listing certain sins as being especially censurable, leaving people with the comfortable and deceptive feeling that avoidance of such sins leaves one largely free from worldliness.

Whatever churches or religious leaders might say about amusements, R.B.'s son Klaudius had his own ideas of fun. As a high school student he contributed his share of laughs. One prank he played never fails to bring gales of laughter each time it is recalled. It took place one Sunday evening at the manse. R.B. enjoyed relaxing with a group of friends after a strenuous day in the pulpit. He might even treat himself to a good cigar, though he never was a heavy smoker. On this particular Sunday evening some of the members of the LaGrave Avenue church had been invited to the minister's house. As the socially proper group was conversing pleasantly Klaudius suddenly burst into the room with a question for his father. "Dad," he asked, "what makes the ocean roar?" The conversation stopped, and R.B. wondered what might come out of his son's mouth. "Well," said Klaudius, "if you had crabs on your bottom you'd roar too." The guests sat in restrained silence, some of them ready to burst into laughter. Mrs. Kuiper was thoroughly annoyed with her son. Klaudius thought he detected a hint of a grin on his father's face. The father, like son, had a bit of the rogue in him. It has been said that every good preacher has some rascality in him.

Chapter 10

The Making of a Great Preacher

"I once heard him preach a sermon that has always stuck with me. He preached on . . ." Words like these I have heard innumerable times from many different people. And often the sermons referred to were preached thirty or forty or more years ago. There was something about R.B. Kuiper's preaching that left indelible impressions. His sermons had a way of getting under the skin of his hearers. Those who heard him rarely left the church with their spirits as they were when they entered.

Was R.B. Kuiper a great preacher? That adjective "great" should be used sparingly in speaking of those who have entered upon the high calling of the gospel ministry, as Frank Gaebelein has so correctly observed in his foreword to Clarence E. Macartney's autobiography *The Making of a Minister*.[1] Just as Gaebelein had no hesitancy in calling Macartney a great preacher, so I have no hesitancy in calling R.B. Kuiper that. Now that we have completed those chapters that deal with R.B.'s congregational ministry, I want to explore those things that went into the making of this great preacher.

Many people have shared this high opinion of R.B. Kuiper as a preacher. John Vander Ploeg, editor of *The Banner*, wrote as follows at the time of R.B.'s death: "On the pulpit he could be superb. Over and over again he would electrify and hold his hearers spellbound as he expounded and elucidated the great truths of Scripture in a way that made them simple, clear, and tremendously alive. A unique delivery, scintillating wit (he was one of the very few who could make a congregation chuckle without a trace of irreverence), inimitable mannerisms, piercing eyes, crisp speech free from anything trite, the rare ability to dramatize what he had to say, and especially the consuming passion to preach the whole counsel of God—these are the qualities that come to mind as we recall what a powerhouse Rev. R.B. Kuiper could be whenever he got up to preach."[2]

Peter H. Eldersveld, highly regarded radio minister on the Christian Reformed Church's Back to God Hour until his early lamented death in 1965, spoke of R.B. as "one who is tops in this business of preaching."[3] Professor F. Klooster of Calvin Theological Seminary described R.B. as "a powerful preacher of the sovereign grace of God . . . whose sermons the people heard gladly. A master of the art of illustration, his sermons were brisk, challenging and biblical. He was a preacher proud to be Reformed and his enthusiasm was contagious . . . In his own inimitable and persuasive manner, he was a preacher without peer."[4] C. Van Til, distinguished professor of Apologetics at Westminster Theological Seminary, had this to say about R.B.'s preaching: "When I was a student at Calvin College I was among the many students who flocked to Sherman St. Church to hear R.B. . . . . He was even in those early days, a prince among preachers."[5]

What went into the making of this prince among preachers? In his preaching one detected the intense earnestness of a Savonarola, the clarity of thought of a John Calvin, the rugged directedness of a Martin Luther, the dramatic power of a George Whitefield, and the personal urgency of a John Wesley. These names have not been chosen at random. R.B.'s writings and utterances bear testimony to his admiration for all of these men of the pulpit. However, let no one think that he copied any one of them. By no means. A facet of R.B.'s greatness lay in the fact that he was himself and never sought to be other than that as he stood before the scrutiny of his listeners.

Hence there was a patent uniqueness about this preacher. No one preached quite as he did, though some tried. And he preached just like no one else. His pulpit work was not marked by the mellifluous speech that one might expect in a gifted orator. His manner had nothing of the ingratiating quality of the "nice guy" who likes to have all men speak well of him. His public address never left one with the impression that he had mastered a list of rules for good public speaking. And yet, as the record clearly shows, he was exceptionally effective in the pulpit. Among preachers he was a remarkable prince.

His Gifts

A woman who had the intelligence and the background to recognize good preaching addressed a letter to one of America's better theological seminaries asking why the school did not turn out more effective preachers. Among the comments she received in response to her letter was this: Send us men with the gifts and we'll turn out good preachers.

That response was on target. A seminary cannot turn out a superior preacher if the Lord has not endowed the aspiring pulpiteer with excellent gifts. This is quite in line with the great apostle's teaching in I Corinthians 12, Ephesians 4 and I Timothy 4. This is certainly apparent in the case of R.B. Kuiper. He had been endowed with great gifts, and an awareness of this fact is of first order in understanding the man's prowess in the pulpit. What were these gifts? He had a superior mind—sharp, clear, orderly. He was blessed with a vigorous spirit; languor was not part of his being. His sense of humor, wedded to a fine mind, was sparklingly exceptional. There was nothing dull about him. His personality was lustrous, impressive. These gifts were apparent in the captivating intensity with which he preached. In speaking of his native endowments, we must note the fact that he was blessed with a healthy physique.

He had the gifts, no doubt about that. But now we have to ask how these gifts were translated into high achievement. We know only too well and with great sadness that life's byways are littered with the tattered remains of many great gifts. In R.B.'s case we can see quite clearly how God in His providence directed his life so that the end product was something splendid.

His Home

Naturally we look first of all to the home into which Rienk was born and the family that nurtured him. The early chapters of this book have, I trust, left some strong impressions of the role that R.B.'s parents played in his development. The clear-minded father with the piercing eyes was as strong a disciplinarian as he was full of love. He was a truly biblical father. And the mother with the eyes that smiled so much was all mother to her family. They furnished an emotionally secure rootage that gained added importance as the family embarked together on the high adventure of moving to a new world. In that new world they found strength and courage in one another as they had to make many adjustments in their strange new setting. The same was true when the family moved to Chicago, where the home served as a fortress against the jostling forces that characterized the huge, brawling metropolis.

Another highly significant element went into the making of the anchorage that the Klaas Kuiper home was for Rienk and his siblings. This element was not something in addition to what we have described above. This element was interwoven with the emotional fabric of the home. Klaas Kuiper was a Calvinist. He was Reformed in his thinking, in his living, in the depths of his being. To say that means more than saying that Klaas Kuiper held to a set of ideas regarding the teaching of the Bible. He was not a Christian who is described as a person holding to a sheaf of biblical teachings in much the same way that a child might hold a bunch of crayons or sticks in his hand. The governing principles that ruled the home of the patriarch Klaas Kuiper were thoroughly Christian, thoroughly biblical in that these principles encompassed all of life, the life that laughs and the life that weeps, the life that worships and the life that toils, the life that tends to the business at hand and the life that dreams. From the moment he began to breathe, R.B. Kuiper's life and this Reformed way of life were one. And this totality brand of Christianity was his food and drink every hour of his formative years. His later formal theological education was an expansion of the seminal theology he had absorbed in his father's house. In other words, R.B.'s theology was not something added to his life; his theology was his life, from the day he was born to the day of his death.

Here lies the key to so much that was distinctively effective in R.B.'s preaching. To him the preaching of a sermon could never be a routine performance, a job to be got out of the way on the road to punching the clock at quitting time. To him preaching was the discharge of a commitment that came out of the inner parts of his being, a commitment that was both intellectual and visceral. Hence the total concentration and earnestness that characterized his preaching. One of R.B.'s grandchildren whispered to his dad as R.B. was preaching, "Grandpa means it, doesn't he. He really means it, doesn't he." He worked, he sweat, he gave it all he had—in the delivery of the sermon as well as in the preparation. R.B. was in no playful mood just before he had to preach. He was tense. A foolish move in traffic didn't amuse him at such times, nor did jokes, which were usually his cup of tea. An elder whose work was that of school janitor once said that a preacher on entering the pulpit should be like a steam boiler ready to blow its head of steam. That was an apt description of R.B. Kuiper.

Because what he preached was the stuff of life for R.B. Kuiper, his life from its very beginning, he could preach with the freedom and abandon that make for power in the pulpit. There was no hint of affectation in his speech or manner. It was all mint R.B. Kuiper. Also for this reason his preaching was so lively in every sense of the word. Because from the start his life in all of its vibrant fullness was interwoven with his biblical, Calvinistic beliefs, he could so naturally enliven his preaching with apt illustrations that edified and delighted his hearers. With the fusion of life and religion that was the matrix from which he came, there simply could be no false separation between the natural and the spiritual, to use terms that were very much part of his vocabulary. For him faith and life were interlocked. Neither pietism nor secularism had place in R.B. Kuiper's existence. His life and service had to be Reformed, Calvinistic in its richest, most exuberant sense.

His Preaching Model

Blessed is the youth aspiring to the gospel ministry who is privileged to hear good preaching in those years when this aspiration is taking root in his soul. Listening to really effective preaching causes his objective to beckon the more urgently and brightly. R.B. had such an inspiring model—his own father. We have already noted that at the time of the father's retirement

R.B.'s brother Barend described him as a "powerful preacher." What kind of model was the father for his son? Klaas Kuiper's ministry led his son to realize that a preacher must be a person of deep earnestness. Shallowness and superficiality have absolutely no place in a preacher's life and work. The father's grip on the truth of God's Word in strong, positive convictions obviously made its mark on Rienk's life, for on this score the intellectual habits of the two men were markedly similar. Hence R.B.'s detestation of superficiality and sloppy intellectual work in preaching was deep-seated. I recall an occasion when the family attended church and heard a sermon that was seriously lacking in spiritual and intellectual quality. On the way home R.B. lamented, "Is it any wonder that people don't go to church when they have to listen to poor stuff like that?"

The model furnished by Rienk's father had many facets. There was the matter of integrity, a moral stamp that was clearly imprinted on the ministry of both men. Sham or pretense may have no place in the preacher's performance. On one occasion both R.B. and I were present when another minister gave some advice to a man very much troubled by a problem. After the minister had spoken to the distressed individual, he turned to R.B. and said, "Well, I guess that satisfied him." It was clear to me that R.B. did not like what he saw and heard, because it seemed apparent that the minister's concern was to get rid of the man and his problem rather than to deal seriously with his burden.

A closely related facet of the model R.B. had in his father was that of compassion, genuine care for the needs of people. In this family there was no conflict between strict devotion to high principle and the exercise of genuine love. In fact, just because love and compassion were wedded to high principle, there was nothing merely clinical or professional about their compassionate concern for people and their needs. It was the real thing. In both father and son this compassion was especially evident in the way in which they were intensely exercised about the response of their hearers, that they might embrace the gospel truth in Christ that is the only road to blessedness in life, life here and life hereafter. This compassion was directed toward temporal needs as well. Generous Christian hospitality was a hallmark of the R.B. Kuiper home, a hospitality that was often spontaneous and not just of the socially engineered kind. And then there were the special deeds of kindness. I experienced such on countless occasions. So did many others. Among R.B. Kuiper's papers I found evidence that he and Mrs. Kuiper regularly sent gifts of money to a young pastor in New England who was working heroically for the gospel on a very small salary.

There was at least one more way in which Klaas Kuiper served as a model. There may be nothing self-serving about the minister's work in the pulpit or out of it. He is God's representative and in that capacity he must correctly and convincingly convey the truth of God in Christ. Therefore the minister must conduct himself with dignity—not pomposity. No cheap showmanship in speech or manner may draw attention to the man and away from the message he brings. Nothing may trivialize the presentation and claims of the message from God's Word with its terrible urgency. The ministry of the Word may never degenerate into mere entertainment or gimmickry. This too R.B. learned well as he sat for years under his father's ministry.

His Education

R.B. Kuiper had an excellent education, an education that made its own significant contribution to the making of a great preacher. In an earlier chapter we have seen why R.B. attended the Morgan Park Academy with its high academic standards, and the University of Chicago with its impressive faculty gathered with care by president William Rainey Harper. One had to admire the feeling for excellence in education that motivated Rev. Klaas Kuiper to send his sons to the University of Chicago rather than to what was then a very inadequate institution for college training in Grand Rapids. There was positively nothing in the Kuiper family that inclined them to the sometimes appealing but faulty notion that says something is good or adequate just because it is held to or promoted in the name of religion. Being Christian in name or intent may never serve as an excuse for mediocrity. Here again the Kuiper family's devotion to Calvinism shines through. This devotion meant that the controlling concern of religion and life was not one's personal salvation, precious as that was for them. Their thinking was not salvation centered; it was theocentric, centering on the triune God, Creator of all things, the great and sovereign God who "gives all men life and breath and everything else," the God in whom "we live and move and have our being" (Acts 17), the almighty One whose glory is the chief goal of life. "Man's chief end," says a well-known catechism, echoing I Corinthians 10:31, "is to glorify God, and to enjoy Him for ever."[6]

Such sublime teaching translates into a philosophy of education that spurs people to know and understand more and more of God's world and His providential government of it so that the luster of the divine glory may shine the more brightly on an ever broadening spectrum of human experience. Such living and learning to God's glory can be and must be a truly Christian enterprise, with the individual in vital union with the Savior and Lord Jesus Christ and His church. The man who greatly influenced Klaas Kuiper and his family, Abraham Kuyper, articulated this philosophy of education when, on October 20, 1880, he delivered the inaugural address as first rector of the school he founded, the Free University of Amsterdam. One statement of that famous address rang like a bell in the ears of all who felt the impact of this remarkable man and his work. "There is," declared Kuyper, "not an inch of the turf of our human existence of which Christ does not cry out: Mine!"

It was this positive Christian perspective on life that inspired R.B. Kuiper throughout his educational career. Endowed with a keen mind, he was always a superior student pursuing an excellent education. And since he was always governed by the Reformed vision of life that had gripped him from childhood, there could be no unsettling breach between his faith and his learning. To be sure, he had his times of doubt all right. Though he expressed himself positively and even emphatically in his preaching, he never was an insensitive, overbearing dogmatist who kept difficult questions at arm's length. From personal experience I know that he could deal gently and compassionately with students who struggled with problems involving their faith and learning. But, though R.B., like most good students, had his times of doubt and uncertainty, the main stream of his life and

education moved forward to form a preacher who could proclaim the riches of Christ with convincing assurance and a
freedom that demonstrated the power of the faith that guided
his life and his learning.

By later standards R.B.'s education would be regarded as
deficient in such areas as science, psychology and philosophy.
The program of study at the University of Chicago when R.B.
attended it reflected the ability and prestige that president
Harper had in the teaching of Hebrew, Greek and Latin as well
as the prevailing educational climate of the times. However,
R.B.'s education at the University of Chicago and at the University of Indiana equipped him superbly for biblical studies and
theology. His studies in the ancient languages that had so much
to do with forming the roots of western culture also served R.B.
well so that he became a master in the use of language. His
pulpit work and his writings demonstrated his ability to use
language with precision and lucidity. His education in the
classics prepared him for the making of sermons that were
sprinkled with apt references to literature and culture. As
teacher of preachers he decried all carelessness of speech and logic.
Precision of speech was surely for R.B. the handmaid of precision
of thought. Once R.B. and I attended a meeting at which the
speaker made a number of fairly obvious mistakes in English. After
the meeting as we were driving home R.B. grumbled, "That man
can't even talk straight; no wonder he can't think straight."

A young woman who had heard R.B. preach expressed her
delight at what she had heard. "I like him," she said; "he's
down to earth. He said, 'Some people perspire, but I sweat.' "
There was an earthy quality about R.B.'s speech. "That's a lotta
hooey" is an expression I have heard many times from him as he
spoke of some comment or proposal that he regarded as inane.
Although he had received a superior education in the classical
languages, his speech was never heavily academic. He had no patience with preachers or other speakers who seemed to delight in
glittering displays of verbiage. An overriding concern with him
was that a spokesman for the Lord must preach so that people
get the message, a message fraught with awesome implications
for eternal splendor or tragedy. Anyone who heard R.B. Kuiper
preach rarely, if ever, left the church wondering what the
preacher meant.

Certain factors in R.B.'s development readily come to mind as combining to produce this preacher with the clear, direct and strong speech. He learned from his father that a preacher is Christ's ambassador, and no self-serving manner of speech might violate that fact. He had grown up in a lively family where the give-and-take among the siblings could hardly allow one to become a "stuffed shirt" with pedantic speech. He became a young man in Chicago, and this bustling, mundane metropolis certainly did not encourage the use of what a teacher of mine called "fine language." Furthermore, R.B. had rubbed shoulders with fellow workers in the vegetable fields of South Chicago and in the huge Pullman plant. All of these contacts with plain people helped R.B. develop a feeling for the common touch. When I was a student of his at Westminster Theological Seminary he commented on my use of rather academic language in my classroom preaching, language I was disposed to use because of the prominence of subjects like philosophy and psychology in my schooling. He told me that I would most likely improve on this score as I mingled with church people who worked at their day-to-day jobs. "A man who sells cars for a living," he told me, "can't afford to use fancy language."

His Wife

R.B. Kuiper had a good wife. For a preacher a good wife is more than a good wife; she is a treasure. Marie Janssen Kuiper was intelligent and had a good education for her time. She had been a successful teacher and principal. She maintained an attractive and orderly home, something of no little importance in a successful preacher's life. She tended to her husband's personal needs. The skinny student she married took on a much healthier appearance after just a few years of Marie's cooking. She was immensely proud of him and did all she could to keep him in robust health. Mrs. Kuiper was also a gracious and generous hostess, and the home's ambience was pleasant. Social amenities were well tended to at the Kuiper manse. With regard to her generosity, R.B. sometimes said that if he didn't watch his wife she would give away everything they owned. I have spoken to several people who as members of the armed forces during

World War II enjoyed the kind hospitality of the Kuiper home in Philadelphia, some of them repeatedly.

Mrs. Kuiper had leadership qualities of her own. When R.B. was president of Calvin College she served as president of the large Women's Missionary Union of the many Christian Reformed churches in and around Grand Rapids. She taught Bible classes for younger and older women's groups in the churches her husband pastored. She taught a Bible class for faculty and student wives at Westminster Seminary. She was also a knowledgeable theologian in her own right. I recall an occasion when she heard a seminary student speak on the subject of infant baptism. The student said that infants of Christian families became members of the church at the time of their baptism. She gently pointed out that this was in error, that in her judgment children born in a Christian home are by that very fact members of Christ's church, and baptism is a sign of that membership in Christ and His church. Marie was, therefore, a great help to her husband. This was especially the case in his writing of books and articles. He submitted everything he wrote to her so that she might detect any grammatical inaccuracy or perhaps some infelicitous use of words. She was a reliable proof-reader too; what a help she was in this exacting exercise. R.B. often said, with respect to one's marriage partner, that every person gets just about what is coming to him. Sometimes I responded to this by saying that his remark was about the most conceited thing he ever said. Of course, that comment didn't do any harm to my standing with my mother-in-law.

A seminary student who as a child had heard R.B. preach listened to a tape recording of a sermon by R.B. on his favorite theme, Salvation by Grace. At the conclusion of the sermon the student exclaimed with some excitement, "That's strong preaching; every word is strong."

That was R.B. Kuiper. His preaching was strong, every word of it. The hearers could not escape the power of the message, the force of his logic, the persuasiveness of his speech, the sharpness of his illustrations, his intense earnestness, his piercing eyes, his delicate sense of humor. The listener had been challenged to hear and to heed the Word of God, challenged powerfully, challenged inescapably. That was the impact of a sermon by R.B. Kuiper. He was a great preacher. The God whose matchless grace in Christ he proclaimed so eloquently caused all things to work together to make him that way.

Chapter 11

College President

College days are memorable days. They are times of high seriousness and delightful madness, times of strenuous study and great fun. In those days young people become men and women. Minds are stretched and talents ripen marvelously. And the vision of life extends far.

A college president has the privilege of witnessing and giving a measure of guidance to the rich experiences unfolding on the campus. The position calls for a person with a sharp mind, great capacity for understanding and growth, and fine sensitivity to the feelings and needs of faculty members and students. When the college is a Christian school, the president must be a person with solid and highly articulate commitment to the principles governing the institution.

From what has gone before in this book it should be apparent that R.B. Kuiper met these requirements to a high degree. This Phi Beta Kappa man from the University of Chicago and other institutions of learning surely had the academic qualifications. His commitment to Calvinism with its sweeping vista of life was beyond question. He had a record of good rapport with children and young people. And his years as a pastor in different settings made him thoroughly aware of the attitudes of the church school's supporting constituency. In the providence of God R.B. became president of Calvin College in 1930. How altogether fitting that one of Rev. Klaas Kuiper's sons should hold this position. The father had so much to do with the founding of the college.

R.B. had taken a leave of absence from the LaGrave Avenue Church one year before in order to join the founding faculty of Westminster Theological Seminary in Philadelphia.[1] Under considerable pressure he had agreed to serve the new school for one year as Professor of Systematic Theology. He confidently expected to return to the ministry at LaGrave, but the appointment to the presidency of Calvin College intercepted his intentions. This was a call he could hardly reject.

It was during R.B.'s tenure as president that I came to know the man who had been only a name to me previously. I was at Calvin for two of the three years that he was there. Calvin College and Seminary had moved to a new campus on Franklin Street in 1917. The combined schools were no longer in the building whose dedication R.B. had witnessed as a boy of seven. The years 1930 to 1933 were a relatively peaceful time. No major theological issues confronted the Christian Reformed Church. These were the great depression years. Everyone was much too busy contending with poverty to afford the luxury of grand controversies. We were all poor. The student who owned a car was a rarity. We walked. The college was small then, numbering under 400 students. We were like a large family, living and studying and enjoying life on a simpler scale. The president was often seen walking to and from his home about a quarter mile from the college, and he always met you with a friendly smile and a pleasant word. He was not an aloof person and participated heartily in campus activities. He enjoyed the fun and excitement of the annual Soup Bowl, a day of festivity and games that served as a mixer for old and new students at the beginning of the academic year. And you almost always saw him at the basketball games, sometimes at the out-of-town games. Basketball was the leading intercollegiate sport at Calvin at that time.

Inaugural

On September 4, 1930, R.B. Kuiper entered upon his duties as president of Calvin College with an inaugural address. He spoke with his characteristic directness and clarity. "Calvin College is not just another college," said the new president. He went on to say, "Calvin College is not just another small college. I say it with equal emphasis, Calvin College is not just another Christian college among the several Christian colleges that dot the face of the land. Calvin College is precisely, pronouncedly, distinctively, a Calvinistic institution. Here I make bold to say that, if it were not for this fact, I should not be standing before you in my present capacity. But for this fact, I should not have the slightest interest in the presidency of this school or in any other position that it might have to offer." Calvin's task, said President Kuiper, is to defend, declare and develop the precious treasure that it has. To do that requires the steadfastness to withstand criticism, often withering criticism. "It will be said of us that we are hopelessly behind the times. We shall sneeringly be called ignoramuses." Then he laid down the challenge to the Calvin College community of scholars and students, "To endure such criticism requires heroism. Was it Chesterton who said: 'Anybody can be a martyr, but it takes a hero to be a fool?' There lurks in every human soul a secret longing for martyrdom, but everybody dreads being styled a fool. Yet fools for God's sake we shall have to be."[2]

The president had a special word for the students as he said, "The students may not be content with being Calvinites. They too must be Calvinists. Keep close to God! Place God at the very center of your life! Do your studying and playing alike to His glory! And if at times you find your work hard, as I trust you will, then remember the words of Henry Ward Beecher: 'They tell us that Calvinism plies men with hammer and chisel. It *does*; and the result is monumental marble. Other systems leave men soft and dirty; Calvinism makes them of white marble, to endure forever.' "

These were strong, resolute words, words truly expressive of R.B.'s deepest and dearest convictions. He would learn in his three years as college president that even among faculty members who subscribe to such high tenets there is not always agreement as to just how these Calvinistic principles are to be applied in every area of learning and culture. It is not always clear just how academic pursuit and confessional loyalty can pull together. A reading of Timmerman's *Promises To Keep*[3] makes plain that tensions turning around this problem have marked much of the school's history. Are such tensions the inevitable accompaniment of a genuine liberal arts academic program that is based on strong religious commitment? It would seem so. But these tensions can be kept under control and can even stimulate growth under strong and wise leadership. This was the case under R.B. Kuiper's presidency. His devotion to Calvinism with its assertion of Christ's claim on all of life had breadth and depth, due in part to his own excellent education. At the same time he was blessed with wisdom. Timmerman, who was a student at the college at the time of Kuiper's presidency and was a member of the faculty for many years after 1945, speaks as follows about R.B., "His enlightened common sense, wit, insight, spiritual force, and dynamic preaching are remembered with gratitutde."[4]

Another source of tension and even irritation during R.B.'s years as Calvin's president was the matter of movie attendance. In 1928 R.B. was member of a committee which issued a report on Worldly Amusements in which movie attendance, dancing and card-playing were singled out. In a previous chapter we noted that R.B. was unhappy with the way the church generally viewed that report. He saw that for many in the church the report encouraged legalism in seeking to enforce proper conduct in the face of certain temptations to worldliness. Rigidly legalistic attitudes were far removed from R.B. Kuiper's character, and he saw that such attitudes simply didn't work with young people generally. He probably suspected that his own son, a student at the college, attended the movies on occasion. He may have heard of the instance (he surely heard of it later on) in which, as his son was trying to slip unnoticed down the aisle of a motion picture theater, a fellow student in the audience called out, "Hi, Kuiper!" R.B. favored the development of an attitude of careful selectivity under strong commitment to Christ in the use of what the world has to offer in books, music, drama or films.

The Great Depression

The most pressing problem R.B. had to face in those three years was financial. The great depression of the thirties was hard on private educational institutions. R.B. wrote about the problem in an article entitled *A Few Financial Facts*.[5] He disclosed that the year 1931 had been difficult for the school. Expenses for the year exceeded income by $22,000. Each family in the Chris-

tian Reformed Church was asked to contribute $3.50 per year to
Calvin College and Seminary—a figure set in 1920 by the synod.
Yet even this relatively small amount (about six cents per week)
many families found hard to give in that time of financial crisis.
The article also stated that the faculty members were returning
ten percent of their already meager salaries.

R.B.'s handling of the crisis won the acclaim of many. Even
the secular press joined in expressing praise for R.B.'s performance during those hard times. The following editorial appeared in the *Grand Rapids Press* of June 5, 1933 as Kuiper's
college presidency came to an end.

KUIPER LEAVES CALVIN

Rev. R.B. Kuiper leaves the presidency of Calvin college
after three years of distinguished service to the local school to
rejoin the faculty of Westminster Seminary at Philadelphia,
responding to repeated pleas from the eastern institution. His
administration has been remarkable for continued progress in
spite of adverse economic circumstances.

Taking over the guidance of the college in 1930 at the
beginning of a period that has proved extremely trying for all
privately supported institutions, President Kuiper has kept
Calvin holding its own. Under him the enrollment has reached
the highest point in history and Calvin's reputation for
scholarship and high educational standards has been maintained. Facing a threatening financial situation he succeeded in
cutting costs almost in half—an example to public as well as
private education.

Previous to his role as educator, in his many years as
preacher here, Dr. Kuiper became known as a brilliant and
forceful speaker and popular leader. His invigorating personality, shown in both official and personal contacts, has
won him the lasting confidence and respect of his colleagues
on the faculty, the student body, the supporters of the school
and the public at large. Calvin college has been fortunate in
having a head so competent to deal with the difficult administrative problems of the past few years and one who leaves
the school in a condition decidedly better for his having been
there.

The Impact of Clear Thinking

The able handling of the college's financial crisis was not President Kuiper's greatest positive contribution in those years. One of his finest contributions was a course he taught in Reformed Doctrine. Many former students have testified that this course more than any other clarified and firmly established their religious and intellectual commitment. The course was a model of clear thinking and orderly presentation. Typical of the many comments about this course that I have heard and read is this testimony by a former student who became an able minister in the Christian Reformed Church, "He taught me Reformed Doctrine while he was president of the college and he shaped my convictions for life."[6]

Those enrolled at Calvin College were not the only college students to benefit from R.B. Kuiper's clear thinking. In February of 1931 R.B. was chosen president of the Board of Trustees of the League of Evangelical Students, an organization founded some six years earlier for the purpose of pressing the claims of orthodox Christianity on college campuses. R.B. held this position for some ten years. Many a student was blessed by the witness of this sharp-minded Christian leader. A speech like "Just What Is Christianity?" delivered at the League conven-

Calvin College when R.B. was President.

tion in 1931, sparkles with plain language, apt illustration and clearly drawn lines. In the address R.B. did what he said he would do: "In this address I shall try, popularly put, 'to come down to brass tacks.' "[7]

College Pranks

No account of college life over a three year period would be complete without some account of the pranks committed by the students. This is especially the case because the president himself had such a great sense of fun. He even wished that some student would pull off a certain prank, as he said more than once in later years. He said he wished at times that some student would leave a cabbage on the platform at chapel time, for such action would give him the chance to say, "It seems that some student has lost his head." To his keen regret he never got the chance to use that choice line.

One of the high jinks carried out by the students brought R.B. amusement that he found hard to restrain. A lady professor became increasingly annoyed at the repeated tardiness of some of the students in her class. So one day she locked the door on the latecomers. But the tardy students were not deterred. They got a ladder and climbed into the second-floor classroom through the window. The professor viewed their entry with shocked outrage and immediately after class marched to the president's office to report the incident. As she was describing what had happened, R.B. turned his back to the irate professor and looked out the window in order to hide the smile he could not suppress. What punishment was meted out to the enterprising scholars is not known.

The interplay of two student escapades had all the marks of an intriguing scenario. Four male students got into the dormitory kitchen one night and helped themselves to the fruit they found in the cooler. One of the four worked in the kitchen and had left a window unlatched. They had planned their clandestine operation well and concocted what seemed to be flawless alibis. That very same night a smudge pot had been left smoldering in a wastebasket in a student's room as the occupant was sleeping. The student woke up coughing and gasping for breath.

The smudge pot prank with its threat to life and safety went too far and called for prompt action. The next morning a suspect was called into the president's office. He was one of the four who had broken into the kitchen to steal the fruit. With his piercing eyes fixed intently on the very uncomfortable student before him, the president bore down on him with these words, "Tell me all about it. Tell me what you did last night. I know the whole story; now let me hear what you have to say." The student was hard pressed. Their alibis had been so airtight. But what if the president knew? He didn't want to be caught lying. He broke down and told the president something he knew nothing about—the stealing of the fruit. (He had not been involved in the smudge pot incident.) He spilled the whole story, including the names of his three partners. When the thoroughly chastened student left the president's office, he set out at once to find the three buddies to tell them what had happened. He found only one of them. One of the other two was called into the president's office and was asked about the raid on the cooler. The student, banking on his sure alibi, denied having any part in the caper. President Kuiper gave the student a withering look and growled, "N---, you're a liar!"

The case of the pilfered fruit had a fascinating sequel. When the Christmas holidays came there were a few students in the dormitory who were unable to make the trip to their homes. (The dormitory was for male students; there was no housing on the campus for women at that time.) President and Mrs. Kuiper invited this group of young men to their home for a social evening to help relieve any loneliness these students might feel. Two of this group of students were involved in the fruit incident. During the evening at the president's home the guests were repeatedly asked to help themselves to fruit that was passed to them in bowls. Fruit, fruit and more fruit—that was the centerpiece of that pleasant social affair at the Kuiper house. As the guests departed that night, R.B. stood at the door with a bowl in each hand, urging the students to take home some fruit. To one of the culprits in the fruit-stealing caper R.B. said, "Have some more fruit; you like it, I know."

R.B.'s three years as president of Calvin College went rather well. One reason may well be that this forthright spokesman for Calvinism understood that this religious commitment covers the whole of life, also humor and laughter.

A Talk to Graduates

Another facet of the character of this many-sided man was revealed in a little talk he gave to a graduating class shortly before commencement day. The substance of his remarks was as follows.

> You are about to become college graduates. This is an important time in your lives. May it be a very happy time for you. The parents of many of you will be coming here to share this wonderful occasion with you. I want you to give your parents a good time. Maybe they won't be dressed just the way you might like them to be. Remember, these are depression days and they have sacrificed, some of them greatly, to put you through college. And maybe they won't speak the English language quite as you might wish them to. Don't you let these things interfere in any way with their happy visit here. I hope you will introduce them to your friends and to your professors. And don't let anyone feel, least of all your parents, that you are anything but immensely proud of them.

The same quality that shines through in these remarks to the graduates came to my attention years after college days. When I was a student at Calvin I used to wonder why the president's daughter was not a member of a rather prestigious women's club that went by the name of K.K.Q., initials which stood for Kalvin Kulture Questers. The male students impishly called them Knock Kneed Queens. The club members were often from more prominent or well-to-do families and the purpose of the group was mainly social. R.B.'s daughter was invited to join the club but she had declined, I learned many years later. She declined out of respect for her father's wishes. He bore no ill will against the individual members of the club, but he did not wish his daughter to be part of an organization that gave even a suggestion of snobbishness. The president sometimes said that there were two classes of people he did not care to see on the campus. They were snobs and slobs. By the latter he meant lazy and careless students. R.B. Kuiper plainly had little time for such.

Chapter 12

Westminster

The summer of 1929 was not the usual kind of summer at the parsonage of the LaGrave Avenue Christian Reformed Church. Yes, there was the welcome change of pace as the hectic schedule of church activities dropped off for a few months. But a new and most unexpected challenge broke in on the delightful respite from a busy church life. The phone rang a lot—long distance calls. And there was a very special guest at dinner, a guest who also listened to R.B. as he preached.

That special guest was none other than one of the most celebrated theologians in the world—Dr. J. Gresham Machen of Princeton Seminary. He came to Grand Rapids to lay before R.B. Kuiper a matter of great urgency. A new theological seminary would be starting in September of that very year in the city of Philadelphia, and Kuiper had been singled out as the man to teach Systematic Theology at the new school. Machen described to R.B. how a reorganization of the board at Princeton Theological Seminary had put the forces of compromise and inclusivism in control, so that the school could no longer be the bastion of Calvinistic theology that it had always been.[1] Because of these developments several of the faculty members felt they could not continue to teach at Princeton and remain true to their convictions. The noted Old Testament scholar Robert Dick Wilson and the able Oswald T. Allis (also an Old Testament scholar) were also leaving Princeton to join the new movement in Philadelphia. Cornelius Van Til, a Christian Reformed pastor, had taught Apologetics at Princeton with marked success in the year just past,[2] but felt he could not remain under the new setup, and had returned to his pastorate at

109

Spring Lake, Michigan; the new seminary hoped to get Van Til for its faculty. They had wanted to get Caspar Wistar Hodge of Princeton to teach Systematic Theology, but he had declined. He just couldn't leave Princeton. There had been a member of the Hodge family on the faculty of the seminary since almost the founding of the school. When Hodge had been asked who might be tapped for teaching the important subject of Systematic Theology, he had said that a Christian Reformed man would be desirable. Then he added that of the Christian Reformed men who had studied at Princeton R.B. Kuiper had made the deepest impression on Dr. B.B. Warfield as a person of scholarship and unqualified devotion to the Reformed faith.

So Machen pressed the issue with R.B. Machen was a charming man, a truly Christian gentleman with keen intellect, articulate persuasiveness, and a devotion to the Calvinistic faith that was free from all cant or superficiality. In his period of hesitation about opening a new seminary he had written in a private letter, "Only a few men have even the slightest inkling of what scholarship is."[3] This man was an able advocate of his cause.

His efforts were of no avail, it seemed. R.B. gave the matter serious consideration and then decided he could not leave his pastorate. Word came that Van Til had also declined. So at the beginning of September the well-rounded faculty that had been so carefully planned was far from a reality. Machen and Allis went to Michigan to get Van Til to change his mind. He too wanted to remain in his Christian Reformed pastorate. But Machen with characteristic tenacity did not give up. The upshot was that when the school opened its doors in late September of 1929 both Kuiper and Van Til were there. Kuiper had stipulated that he would help out the new school for just one year. His family did not accompany him to Philadelphia in 1929.

The Opening of Westminster

Fifty students were enrolled at Westminster Theological Seminary when it opened on September 25, 1929. This number is particularly remarkable in view of the fact that the determination to establish a new seminary was not made until July 18,

1929. There were good reasons for this surprising enrollment at a school whose existence had been decided upon less than three months before. Two members of the founding faculty had reputations as world-renowned biblical scholars, namely, Robert Dick Wilson and J. Gresham Machen. Machen's name was a special magnet. He was easily the leading spokesman of conservative Christianity in America. His book *Christianity and Liberalism*, published in 1923, had positively established his reputation as Christianity's most articulate voice in the land if not in the world. His book *What Is Faith?*, appearing in 1925, reinforced this high standing. His earlier book *The Origin of Paul's Religion* had been widely acclaimed as the work of a first-rate scholar. Furthermore he enjoyed a high degree of popularity as a teacher. His biographer informs us that "he was regarded, in the late twenties at least, as the most interesting and successful teacher" at Princeton Seminary.[4] Of no small importance in the founding of Westminster was the element of publicity. The beginning of the school together with the long parade of events that led up to it were well publicized in leading newspapers and religious magazines throughout the country.

The fifty students, about evenly distributed among the three seminary classes, were greeted by a highly competent faculty. To the core group of Wilson, Machen, Allis, Kuiper and Van Til were added Paul Woolley in Church History (he also served most effectively as Secretary and Registrar), Allan A. MacRae in Old Testament and Ned B. Stonehouse in New Testament. The added strength in the Old Testament department was called for due to Wilson's age; he died in the seminary's second year. The Practical Theology department was manned through makeshift arrangements involving part-time teaching by some able ministers until Kuiper occupied the chair in 1933.

Machen gave the main address at the opening exercises of the new seminary. He spoke on "Westminster Theological Seminary: Its Purpose and Plan." He made crystal clear what would be the outstanding feature of the new school, namely, its uncompromising commitment to the Scriptures, God's own infallible Word, as the basis and guide for all the instruction. In the same breath he declared that such devotion to the Bible means faithful adherence to "that system of theology, that body of truth, which we find in the Bible . . . the Reformed Faith, the

Faith commonly called Calvinism, which is set forth gloriously in the Confession and Catechisms of the Presbyterian Church."[5] This resolute allegiance to the Reformed faith many supporters of the new seminary did not fully comprehend. Not a few of them were really Fundamentalists, people who were truly devoted to the Bible as the very Word of God but were not equally devoted to the Reformed faith as the system of truth taught in the Bible. Machen was of one mind with these fellow Christians in their insistence on the inviolability of "fundamentals" like the inerrancy of Scripture, the virgin birth of Christ, the substitutionary atonement, Christ's bodily resurrection, and the reality of biblical miracles. In the battle against the forces of unbelief he stood shoulder to shoulder with the Fundamentalists.

But he didn't like the term Fundamentalist and did not choose to be known by that name. How he felt on this sensitive issue is made quite plain in a letter he wrote declining the invitation to become the first president of a projected Bryan Memorial University to be established at Dayton, Tennessee. This invitation was one of several Machen received when his position at Princeton was becoming increasingly dubious. In his letter declining the invitation Machen stated, "Nevertheless, thoroughly consistent Christianity, to my mind, is found only in the Reformed or Calvinistic Faith; and consistent Christianity, I think, is the Christianity easiest to defend. Hence I never call myself a 'Fundamentalist.' There is, indeed no inherent objection to the term; and if the disjunction is between 'Fundamentalism' and 'Modernism,' then I am willing to call myself a Fundamentalist of the most pronounced type. But after all, what I prefer to call myself is not a 'Fundamentalist' but a 'Calvinist'—that is, an adherent of the Reformed Faith. As such I regard myself as standing in the great central current of the Church's life—a current which flows down from the Word of God through Augustine and Calvin, and which has found noteworthy expression in America in the great tradition represented by Charles Hodge and Benjamin Breckinridge Warfied and the other representatives of the 'Princeton School.' I have the warmest sympathy with other evangelical churches and a keen sense of agreement with them about those Christian convictions which are today being most insistently assailed."[6]

This kindly feeling toward non-Calvinist evangelical groups came through in Machen's opening address in these carefully chosen words, "We rejoice in the approximations to that body of truth (Calvinism) which other systems of theology contain; we rejoice in our Christian fellowship with other evangelical churches; we hope that members of other churches, despite our Calvinism, may be willing to enter into Westminster Seminary as students and listen to what we have to say. But we cannot consent to impoverish our message by setting forth less than what we find the Scripture to contain . . . Glorious is the heritage of the Reformed Faith. God grant that it may go forth to new triumphs even in the present time of unbelief!"[7]

It was this forthright and unabashed avowal of Calvinism that drew Kuiper and Van Til to Westminster, even more so than did the persistent pleadings of Machen. These men felt very much at home in this openly Reformed atmosphere as strong confessional commitment was coupled with high standards of scholarship. In this setting of biblical and creedal fidelity at a high level was a spirit of mutual respect among the faculty members. They were not of one mind on all matters, as, for example, on the details of Christ's second coming. And it soon became apparent that Van Til's approach to Apologetics differed from that of Machen. But there was never any hint of petty jealousy or criticism among these high-minded men. They were engaged in a struggle for the true biblical faith, and they stood side by side under a powerful sense of mission, with lesser concerns submerged.

A Confidential Letter

As he had stipulated, after one year R.B. left Westminster to return to Grand Rapids, to the presidency of Calvin College and not to the pastorate at LaGrave church, as he had expected. In the three years of his college presidency he did not forget Westminster. The cause had made a place for itself in his life. This was demonstrated by articles he wrote about Westminster. In October of 1932 he wrote "Modernism and We,"[8] an article in which he indicated his distress at the lack of serious interest in the Westminster struggle on the part of so many in the Christian

Reformed Church. The next spring he wrote "Westminster Versus Princeton—A Doctrinal Issue."[9] The joining of the Board of Directors and the Board of Trustees at Princeton was not just a matter of administrative housekeeping, as some people claimed. The reorganization meant a serious weakening of the historical biblical and Calvinistic stance of the seminary, R.B. argued, as indicated by the presence on the new board of two men who had signed the thoroughly modernistic Auburn Affirmation.[10] R.B. also had no patience with explanations of what happened at Princeton which attributed the break to alleged intolerance and belligerence on the part of Machen, or which dismissed the whole matter by saying that Machen could not walk on the same campus with Professor Charles R. Erdman, who had aligned himself with the views and policies of President J. Ross Stevenson.

Westminster Seminary did not forget R.B. Kuiper. They very much wanted this gifted man back again. How the Westminster people felt about R.B. is revealed in a confidential letter Machen sent to him less than a year after he had returned to Grand Rapids. Since the letter, dated March 16, 1931, says much about Westminster, Machen and Kuiper, it is here reproduced in full.

Dear Kuiper:

I am writing to you about Westminster Seminary in a completely confidential way that would be quite impossible except for the unbounded trust that I repose both in your discretion and in your devotion to the Seminary.

The year has passed in some respects in a satisfactory manner. Despite the business depression, the funds have been coming in sufficiently to meet the necessary expenses, and prospects for the future are as good as could be expected. We have also a good student body, slightly larger than that of last year.

But it has been becoming painfully evident that something is very seriously lacking in the life of the institution. Disruptive tendencies among the students—an exaggerated and somewhat legalistic objection to certain forms of amusement, militant premillennialism, an unhealthy pietism and anti-intellectualism, desire for "English Bible", etc.—while not as yet rampant, have been making themselves felt in increasing measure, and were even expressed the other day in a contest (unsuccessful, it is true) for the presidency of the student association.

These tendencies were all present last year, but were held in check very largely through the influence of one man. That man is the present president of Calvin College. Your true and fervent piety, your real devotion to the Reformed Faith, your delightful and cordial relations with the students, your signal success as a preacher and as a teacher, and your sound common sense coupled with a saving sense of humor—these were the things which more than any other kept the student body in a healthy condition.

Frankly, we do not see how in the world we are going to do without you. It is perfectly evident that a professor of homiletics must be secured. The present arrangement cannot possibly continue, for various reasons. We have canvassed various possibilities during the year, but no solution of the problem has come to us. I am convinced that if we obtain an incumbent in this all-important position who has only a vague acquaintance with the Reformed Faith, we shall at once have a rift in our institution which will be fatal. That consideration rules out a good many names. The plain fact is that in the Presbyterian Church in the U.S.A. there is not one single preacher of the kind that we really need. My mind has gone over and over the possibilities until I feel almost distracted. I have also thought of men in other churches but as yet I cannot find one who really at all would meet our need.

After a year of consideration, we talked the matter over last Saturday informally but very earnestly in the Faculty. Various possibilities were considered, but without avail. In this condition of mind, we thought of one thing. It seemed to be presumptuous for us to think of it at all, but to save our lives we could not get it out of our minds. We all feel, namely, that if you could come back to us after your two year term at Calvin College is over—the term for which I believe you are technically obligated—the problem would be solved in the only really satisfactory manner, and the institution would go on to really great things.

I know very well that you are making a splendid success in your present position. It seems, therefore, almost absurd for us to come to you with the suggestion that is implied in what I have just said. But when a man is out there drowning in the water at Atlantic City, in accordance with your illustration of the other night, he is apt to reach out without undue modesty for whatever life line may be at all in sight. I can only say that if you did come back to us, I think you would be performing a service absolutely unique in the whole realm of the Reformed churches. I cannot possibly imagine a life work more splendid. We have a glorious opportunity, and I do feel that we are in very great danger of failing to meet it for the lack of what you alone could give us.

If you could come to us after this next year, we all feel that we should certainly wait for you, and I am writing to you to that effect at the express instance of all the members of the Faculty.

It is quite needless for me to say that what I have told you about the condition of Westminster Seminary is in the very strictest confidence. I felt in writing to you that I was in the presence of a friend with whom any reserve as to the real situation would be altogether unnecessary and out of place. All that I can do is to present to you our profound need and the wonderful possibilities which your presence at Westminster Seminary would mean for the cause that we all love so dearly. Will you not let us know, with a frankness equal to mine, how the matter lies in your mind?

Cordially yours,

J. GRESHAM MACHEN

R.B. Returns to Westminster

R.B. did not return to Westminster after two years, but he did return after three. In May of 1933 the Board of Trustees of Westminster Seminary appointed R.B. Kuiper to the chair of Practical Theology. "The election was by written ballot and was unanimous," the secretary of the board wrote in apprising R.B. of the appointment. The communication from the board, written by Harold S. Laird, went on to say, "Although this is a formal intimation, let me hasten to add that very deep enthusiasm concerning your election was manifested at the meeting of the board. It was a largely attended meeting and this invitation to you to accept our election comes to you with all the earnestness and fervor which we can command . . . I can only emphasize again how deeply eager and anxious we all are that you may accept this election . . . Dr. Macartney presided at the commence-

ment exercises and when he made public announcement of your
election it was inspiring to see the thrill of joy which ran over the
faces of a large number in the audience who know and love
you . . ."

The appointment was accepted and the Kuiper family
moved to Philadelphia the following summer to begin a period
of service continuing until retirement in 1952. This was a spot
where R.B. with his native endowments, his excellent education,
and his experience as a particularly successful preacher and ad-
ministrator could serve with a large measure of personal
satisfaction and distinction. And the colleagues with whom he
labored were all men of exceptional caliber and dedication. R.B.
was very much aware of this fact, as evidenced by some remarks
he made at the time of his inauguration as Professor of Practical
Theology. Before a gathering of trustees, faculty and students
R.B. said, "I count it an honor, a great honor, the greatest
honor of my life, to be associated with so scholarly and so godly
a group of men as that which constitutes the Faculty of
Westminster Theological Seminary."[11] R.B. enjoyed the esteem
and affection of this body of men with their strong devotion to
the faith he embraced so wholeheartedly.

Among these scholars was a new face that had not been
there when R.B. taught at Westminster in the first year of the
school's existence. John Murray, a Scotsman, had taken R.B.'s
place in Systematic Theology when he had left to become president of Calvin College. Murray had been assisting Professor
Hodge at Princeton Seminary, but he no longer felt at home
there after the revamping of the school's board of control. His
coming to Westminster was a great boon to the seminary. He
proved to be a superb teacher in his field. His teaching was
strongly exegetical, so that his students were left with no doubt
as to the thorough scripturalness of the Reformed faith. An
especially warm relationship of affection and respect developed
between Professors Kuiper and Murray. R.B. did not hesitate to
speak of John Murray as the best teacher of Systematic
Theology in the world.

R.B.'s relations with the students were equally amicable.
The intimate and affectionate personal bond that grew between
the students and R.B. was borne out, for instance, in the names
the students often used in speaking of Professor and Mrs.

Kuiper. The two Kuiper children commonly spoke to and about their parents as "Pa" and "Ma," and the students came to adopt these names when speaking about their beloved professor and his wife.

This setting of challenge, united devotion to Calvinism, and mutual appreciation called forth the best R.B. had to offer. The Westminster years were surely some of the most productive of his full life of service. There was at Westminster an electric sense of high purpose in the furtherance of a holy cause, a spirit akin to that which motivated the apostle Paul. Like the man who more than any other was responsible for the rise of Westminster Seminary, namely, J. Gresham Machen, the school stood unashamedly and indefatigably in the front lines of the battle to proclaim and defend that gospel of Jesus Christ in all the power and purity of the saving grace it embodied. So R.B. worked hard. He was not satisfied to develop a few courses which he could simply parrot year after year. He continually developed new material so that those who graduated from the seminary might realize the full scope of the gospel ministry in a church of Reformed persuasion. The broad range of his course offerings remains to be discussed in a later chapter. That the challenges Westminster posed for R.B. quickly enlisted his best efforts is apparent from a remark he made in a letter to his daughter, who was studying at the University of Michigan. The letter, written in January of 1934, contains this commentary on his labors, "I am working about three times as hard this semester as the first, but my salvation lies in the ignorance of the students." One had to know R.B. to understand that this quip said less about the students than it did about the standards he set for himself.

An almost amusing sidelight is cast on the life of the Kuipers in Philadelphia in another letter R.B. sent to his daughter in January of 1934. The daughter, who enjoyed the benefits of a generous scholarship, received a distress call from her father. "We have used our money so fast," wrote R.B., "that we don't see how we're going to finish the month. So please send me a check for $5 at once." In the day in which this book is being written the amount of money R.B. asked for seems too ridiculously small for any helpful purpose. In those days of the Great Depression, when hamburger sold for five cents a pound, five dollars was an encouraging sum of money.

Such passing annoyances took nothing away from the quality of life the Kuipers enjoyed in Philadelphia. The good relations among the faculty members spilled over into pleasant social times as they visited in one another's homes. Machen was often a guest in the Kuiper home and he, being a bachelor, was effusive in his praise of Mrs. Kuiper's home cooking. Then again the Kuipers as well as the other faculty members and more than a few of the students were often the beneficiaries of Machen's generosity as he gave out tickets to Ivy League football games. "Das," as he was called by his friends, had a way of offering these tickets (usually fifty-yard line) that went like this, "Would you do me the favor of taking these tickets off my hands?"[12]

There were happy times when groups of students with their diverse backgrounds enjoyed the warm hospitality of the Kuiper home. Many of the students learned about the amenities of Philadelphia social life as the young men all rose from their seats when a lady was introduced. At such gatherings in the Kuiper home R.B.'s performance as a sparkling conversationalist was matched by the gracious manner of Mrs. Kuiper as hostess. Also contributing to the pleasantness of the Kuiper experience at Westminster were the cultural and scenic offerings of Philadelphia and environs. Significant events in music, drama and lecture were never in short supply. And major league baseball gave R.B. ample opportunity to enjoy his favorite sport. The beauties of Fairmount Park and of springtime in Philadelphia with brilliant displays of rhododendron and dogwood etched scenes that could never fade from memory.

The Kuipers with their six grandchildren.

Five of the six brothers: from left, Herman, R.B., Barend, John, Henry.

Chapter 13

Chairman of the Faculty

Fruitful, personally satisfying—such were the years the Kuipers spent at Westminster. But these years were not without hurt. While R.B. was at Calvin College death took away Robert Dick Wilson, as already noted. He was one of the original faculty members who had left Princeton to found Westminster. After R.B. returned to Westminster another leader in the movement passed away, namely, Rev. Frank H. Stevenson, who had given able guidance as first president of the Board of Trustees. Less than two years later Oswald T. Allis, also one of the three professors who had left Princeton, resigned from the Westminster faculty because of differences of opinion regarding church developments that affected the seminary. His departure was viewed with great regret by Machen and Kuiper as well as by the other members of the faculty, and by the students too.[1]

Then there were highly disruptive tensions growing out of the fact that all those who joined hands in the establishment of Westminster over against the changed Princeton were not really united in their understanding of the Reformed witness of the seminary. Intense struggles broke out over questions relating to the second coming of Christ, dispensationalism, and the meaning of Christian liberty in matters of food and drink. An outgrowth of these conflicts was the resignation of A.A. MacRae, who then became president of a new school named Faith Theological Seminary, also located in the Philadelphia area. Discussion of struggles surrounding these issues and related matters is appropriately part of the story of another institution, namely, the Orthodox Presbyterian Church, and will appear in the chapter entitled The Presbyterian Churchman.

A Staggering Blow

Of far greater consequence in the life of the seminary was an event that no one in the school community had dreamed of in even his darkest moments. This wholly unexpected event was none other than the death of J. Gresham Machen on January 1, 1937. This was a staggering blow that left everyone associated with the seminary overwhelmed with grief and dismay. Their champion was dead. In the autumn of 1936 Machen had suffered from a cold that would not go away. Troublesome and sticky problems in the church and seminary distressed him a great deal. Then, instead of resting during the holidays at Christmas time, as his family and friends had urged him to do, he went to North Dakota to keep some speaking engagements he felt he had to honor. He never spared himself in the face of what he believed he had to do or what he had committed himself to do. He left for the rigors of the North Dakota winter still troubled by his cold and having as his outer protective garment only a light topcoat. Part of his journey was a sixty-mile stretch in a heaterless car in very cold weather. He quickly became ill. He did not want medical attention until he had fulfilled his speaking engagements. Pleurisy set in. He spoke publicly in great pain but without complaint. Finally, he was hospitalized, though he wanted to return to Philadelphia for treatment. Pneumonia developed and on New Year's Day 1937 this valiant warrior for Christ passed to that perfect blessedness where there are no struggles. Some of the last words he spoke were these, "Isn't the Reformed faith grand."

The writer of this book was in the Kuiper home at the time. They were mournful days as the telephone kept ringing, with each call bringing a message of increasing gravity. When it appeared that we could no longer hope for Machen's recovery, Mrs. Kuiper, who was usually composed, broke into weeping. So much of their lives was wrapped up in this dying man.

This man was an exceptional person. Since he was such a significant influence in R.B. Kuiper's life, a few further words about him are in order. If any one word describes the man, it is the word *integrity*. He could not tolerate any falsity or ambiguity in his beliefs or commitments. As a student at the universities of Marburg and Göttingen in Germany he sat under the teaching of several of Europe's leading biblical scholars, such as Jülicher, Weisse, Herrmann, Bousset, Schürer, Heitmüller and Bonwetsch. Under such men he caught the vision of honest and thorough scholarship. At the same time he went through an intense spiritual struggle involving his continuing allegiance to the faith he had been taught. "The only way," Machen wrote in a letter to his mother, "in which the thinker can hold to the old belief is by piercing below the surface and thus finding that on the merits of the question the old view has the facts on its side. And it is possible to satisfy oneself that one has gotten below the surface and has a right to decide on the merits of the question only by investigating every nook and cranny of both sides of the question."[2]

Machen therefore always spurned easy and simplistic answers to difficult questions. His deep respect for the highest standards is symbolized in the fact that he was a mountain climber of no mean achievement, as evidenced by his conquest of the majestic Matterhorn in the Swiss Alps. His goals and standards were always high. For this reason he postponed his ordination for several years after he began teaching at Princeton in 1906. He wanted to be sure that his ordination met the high standards he held regarding it, and that he was not engaged in some sort of charade or mere ecclesiastical ritual. All of his works and writings were done in the conviction that what he set forth had "the facts on its side." And once he had made his commitment on such high ground, no personal sacrifice was too great in his pursuit of what he believed to be right and true. This was, in the wondrous providence of God, probably the leading reason for his early death at the age of fifty-five, the same age at which death came to his main theological mentor, John Calvin.

These reflections on the character of a man who, next to R.B.'s father, had the greatest influence on Kuiper's career, can best be concluded with a tribute from a quite unexpected source. That source was Pearl S. Buck, noted author and former Presbyterian missionary whom Machen had opposed because of her liberal views. In her highly perceptive tribute she wrote as follows, "We have lost a man whom our times can ill spare, a man who had convictions which were real to him and who fought for those convictions and held to them through every change in time and human thought. There was power in him which was positive in its very negations. He was worth a hundred of his fellows who, as princes of the church, occupy easy places and play their church politics and trim their sails to every wind, who in their smug observance of the convictions of life and religion offend all honest and searching spirits. No forthright mind can live among them, neither the honest skeptic nor the honest dogmatist. I wish Dr. Machen had lived to go on fighting them."[3]

Machen's death was indeed a crushing blow. Faculty members and students went about in a benumbed and dazed state when they returned after the Christmas holidays. Without Dassie the place wasn't the same. But those whom Machen had rallied around his cause were made of sterner stuff than to break under their acute sense of loss. The cause, the seminary, had to go on. Any weakening of resolve or effort would be a rebuke to the memory of their beloved fallen leader. One of the first actions of the faculty was to choose a new chairman, a position Machen had held since the opening of the seminary. There was considerable speculation on the campus as to who might be chosen to this important post. Would it be Dr. C. Van Til, who, having served the school so well and continuously from the start, would be considered the senior member of the staff? The man chosen was R.B. Kuiper. It was reported that Van Til was not interested in the position, feeling with characteristic humility that the administrative duties involved in the position of chairman did not suit whatever gifts the Lord had given him. Van Til was very pleased with the choice of R.B. The latter's clear-cut devotion to the Reformed faith, his acumen and his proved gifts of leadership signalled the selection. Thus with dramatic suddenness R.B. was catapulted into a position in which his great gifts could be used more effectively than ever before.

Moving Forward

Another important forward-looking action was the launching of a campaign which had two goals, namely, the purchase of a new campus and the strengthening of the financial base of the school by setting up a half-million dollar endowment. The second part of the effort was not achieved, but a new campus was purchased. By September of 1937 the seminary had moved to a beautiful twenty-acre estate located just outside of Philadelphia. On September 29, 1937, the spacious main building on the campus was dedicated as the J. Gresham Machen Memorial Hall.

In the following year another positive forward step was taken by the seminary. A new scholarly theological publication appeared under the name *The Westminster Theological Journal*. Edited for the faculty by Professors John Murray and Paul Woolley for the first fifteen years of its long and illustrious career, the journal contributed much to current theological discussion and to Westminster's standing as a center of biblical, Calvinistic learning which recognized its debt to "nineteen centuries of Christian history, thought, and experience" on the one hand, and on the other hand accepted "responsibility to present the Christian faith in the context of the present."[4] The publication was and still is issued in the spring and fall of each year.

These positive steps played their part in insuring, in God's gracious providence, the continued witness of the school. And though the trials the seminary went through in the thirties were severe, the school did weather them in surprisingly good shape. The loss of men like Machen and Allis was most trying. The

Machen Hall, Westminster Theological Seminary.

resignation of MacRae further weakened the Old Testament department. But the appointment of Edward J. Young closed the gap in that phase of instruction. Young in time gained an enviable reputation as an outstanding Old Testament scholar, with his widely-used three-volume commentary on Isaiah as ample evidence of his productivity and biblical erudition. The fact that almost all of the faculty members were relatively youthful was largely responsible for the continuation of a strong and steadfast Reformed witness over many years. To be sure, the magnetism of Machen's name was no longer there to draw students. The student body declined in numbers. In the year 1937 the school had thirty graduates. By 1946 that number had dwindled to five and by 1949 to three. But by the end of the forties and in the early fifties enrollments began to climb and have been increasing ever since, so that by 1984 there were one hundred-nine graduates, among them a grandson of R.B. Kuiper. Through those lean years the solid loyalty to the Reformed faith and to the seminary on the part of the faculty was a tremendous asset. R.B.'s firm and judicious leadership, always exercised with grace and wit, also contributed much to the school's survival and renewed growth.

His teaching and administrative duties, his activities in and for the Orthodox Presbyterian Church together with a busy schedule of speaking and writing kept R.B. well occupied. It was to be expected that he would be in great demand as a preacher in many churches and denominations. He was a popular conference speaker, also for young people. The youth liked his directness and clarity, as well as his sense of humor. His writings were extensive, and their range and subject matter can only be touched on here.[5] Many book reviews came from his pen. They were thorough and critical in the best sense. No book was dismissed with a blurb like "all can learn from this book," or "there are some points (unnamed) with which one can differ." He wrote some significant articles for *The Westminster Theological Journal*. A lengthy treatise on "The Christian Pulpit and Social Problems" (1939) is still profitable reading for the pulpiteer. The same can be said for "Personal Religion Divorced from Objective Christianity" (1944) and "The Word of God Versus the Totalitarian State" (1948). In the last-named article R.B. declared that the reason for the ascendancy of the totalitarian state is "at bottom . . . one of irreligion and false theology."

In 1941-42 R.B. became involved in a doctrinal controversy that touched on a sensitive and important area of Reformed theology. The controversy swirled around utterances and writings of men in the Reformed Church in America in which the guilt of infants before God was denied. Important doctrinal points such as total depravity and the imputation of Adam's sin were at stake. R.B. wrote a booklet entitled *Are Infants Guilty Before God?*[6] To the question why he should involve himself in a dispute occurring in another denomination R.B. had this to say, "Not any one denomination, but the church universal, is custodian of God's revealed truth. As pillar and ground of the truth, the church universal has the task of upholding the truth. The fortunes of Christian doctrine in one Christian church should be of vital concern to every other Christian church. In these days of so much false ecumenicalism this demand of true ecumenicalism may well be stressed."

From almost the very beginning of Westminster Theological Seminary it was apparent that the faculty of the school would be a productive body of scholars. A high standard was set by the appearance in 1930 of Machen's monumental work on *The Virgin Birth of Christ*, a volume on which he had been working for many years. In time other significant works followed, such as C. Van Til's critique of Barthianism in his *The New Modernism* (1946). Especially noteworthy among the writings produced by the Westminster professors in the school's earlier years was a symposium under the title *The Infallible Word*, published in 1946. The authors were John Murray, E.J. Young, N.B. Stonehouse, John H. Skilton, Paul Woolley, R.B. Kuiper and Cornelius Van Til. In producing this symposium the seminary gave to the world a badge by which the school could be especially identified. R.B.'s contribution was entitled "Scriptural Preaching." Since his essay goes into the question of what true scriptural preaching is, further discussion is best reserved for the next chapter.

This body of scholars soon turned its attention to the matter of granting advanced degrees in theology. In about 1942 the school petitioned Pennsylvania's State Council of Education for power to grant the degrees of Master of Theology and Doctor of

Theology. Authorization was given at that time to grant the Master's degree, but power to grant the doctorate was not given at that time. As chairman of the faculty R.B. did a great deal of work in connection with this effort, particularly in seeking authorization to grant the Doctor's degree. The State of Pennsylvania had high standards for its educational institutions, and schools that served as diploma-mills handing out cheap degrees did not find a hospitable climate there. And Westminster did not wish to be known as that kind of school. Westminster's petition was not quickly honored. In fact, the seminary did not gain authorization to grant the doctorate until 1959, seven years after R.B. had retired from Westminster.

Those who graduated from Westminster in the years that R.B. was chairman of the faculty got to hear a speech that may have been largely unintelligible to most of them. As is common practice in most academic institutions, the head of the faculty or his surrogate has the responsibility at commencement exercises formally to present the candidates for graduation as having properly completed the required course of study. This formal official presentation was done by R.B. Kuiper by rendering from memory the customary brief speech in fluent Latin. And the pronunciation of the Latin words and phrases was in purest form, in keeping with R.B.'s excellent education in the classical languages. He completely detested Latin spoken with an American accent. The graduates could feel that this speech in flawless Latin gave to their diplomas an added embellishment.

It was with great regret that Westminster Seminary bade farewell to Professor and Mrs. Kuiper at the time of his retirement in 1952. He was then sixty-six years of age and still in vigorous health. His decision to retire was dictated by a desire to have time to write books that might be of help to the general membership of the church toward growth in the faith that was so precious to R.B. How Westminster Seminary felt about R.B.'s service there is best expressed by an excerpt from a Memorial Minute adopted by the faculty at the time of his death in 1966. The words of this tribute are as follows:

> The faculty pays grateful tribute to the superb contribution made by Professor Kuiper during these twenty years of service to the upbuilding and strengthening of the Seminary

and to the witness which it has by God's grace been able to
render to the whole counsel of God. His career at the Seminary
as in other activities has been marked by unrelenting fidelity to
the Reformed faith. His teaching, as his preaching, was
characterized by clarity of thought, forceful presentation, and
impassioned appeal. A generation of students owe
unmeasured debt to the instruction he so competently imparted, and his colleagues on the Faculty highly appreciate the
benefit derived from his wise counsel and from the well-
balanced and careful scholarship which he exemplified.[7]

R.B. and Mrs. Kuiper in Philadelphia.

Chapter 14

Teacher of Preachers

"Preach so simply that a child can understand you, and then chances are that the older people will understand you too." It is doubtful that any student for the ministry at Westminster between 1933 and 1952 missed this delicious piece of tongue-in-cheek wisdom tinged with humor. With this kind of spicy morsel R.B. Kuiper often enlivened his teaching, so that students rarely complained that his classes were dull.

By this unique bit of instruction R.B. was not encouraging sloth or superficiality in sermonizing. By no means. Elsewhere he had this to say on the subject, "Personally I see no sense in preaching special sermons or even sermonettes for the children. Every sermon should contain a great deal to interest the little ones. The minister who finds it difficult to come down to the intellectual level of children should study harder. It requires less study to preach for adults than for children."[1]

There was nothing in R.B.'s teaching or preaching that in any way suggested that the making of sermons is an easy thing to do. Sermon preparation requires a great deal of study, he made unmistakably clear. He drove this point home by another of his arresting comments. "A good preacher," he told his students, "can produce one good sermon a week. A fair preacher can produce two fair sermons a week. A poor preacher can produce three or more sermons per week, but we'll say nothing about their quality." For R.B. facility in spouting verbiage (he sometimes called it the "gift of gab") had little to do with rendering good sermons, unless that facility was linked to disciplined study and reflection, especially on the precise meaning of the text of Scripture.

Some Important Ground Rules

R.B. Kuiper was Professor of Practical Theology at Westminster. He had some definite ideas about what that title meant. Of first importance was the point that Practical Theology is *theology*. He did not think of his work at the seminary as anything like a glorified assembly line turning out kits containing ten simple tools for becoming a successful preacher. His teaching in no way resembled a popular image of a department of Practical Theology as being little more than a place for learning the techniques of effective pastoral public relations. As we have seen, the great biblical principles that powered the Reformation had captured the full allegiance of his mind and heart. These same principles governed all of his teaching, just as they had governed his work in the churches he served. This fact among others endeared him to his colleagues. They knew he was an able theologian and not merely a homiletical technician.

For him and his colleagues this meant that the teacher and those he taught had to be thorough students of the Bible, well schooled in its original languages. And this R.B. certainly was. For Kuiper and his fellow professors theology did not consist in the spinning of fine scholastic tapestries woven from strands of biblical teaching on the loom of human logic. Rather for them theology was the systematic formulation of the teaching of the Bible with the systematizing principles drawn from the Bible itself. Therefore, if any one rule governed Kuiper's teaching of preachers it was this, "Preach the Word" (II Tim. 4:2).

According to R.B. preaching the Word meant preaching the Word incarnate, that is, Jesus Christ. He constantly stressed the point that every sermon should preach Christ. This was not to be achieved by some reference to Christ added on to a sermon in an artificial way, much as a noted preacher once issued an altar call at the end of a sermon that had said nothing about the only way of salvation in Christ. The message of the gospel is the good news of full salvation through Christ and His shed blood, and therefore the preacher of the gospel must always preach Christ in the context of the whole of Scripture's teaching. The preacher must be under the same compulsion as the great apostle who cried out, "Woe is me if I do not preach the gospel" (I Cor. 9:16). It hardly needs saying that for the apostle Paul preaching the gospel meant preaching Christ (I Cor. 2:12).

At the same time R.B. instructed his students that the gospel in its essential message of salvation in the Cross of Christ must always be made crystal clear. The preacher is dealing with people whose eternal destiny depends on the preaching of the Word (Rom. 10:8-15). The high seriousness of preaching demands that the way of salvation be set forth with total clarity. Poor preparation, sloppy presentation, abstruse academic language, lack of an overwhelming sense of mission, personal hypocrisy—none of these things on the part of the minister may interfere with the clear call from the pulpit to turn from sin and the emptiness of the world to the sure riches of grace and glory in Christ. R.B.'s own preaching with its sparklingly clear and impassioned presentation of the gospel of saving grace in the Cross of Christ was the student's best example of what the professor of Practical Theology was teaching him.

"Get On Your Hind Legs and Preach"

Since the preaching of the gospel is a matter of such high seriousness and importance, the preacher must give it his best. A sermon is not a social chat, nor is it an after-dinner speech, nor is it a formal lecture, nor is it an academic discourse. It is something quite different from and also much more than any of these. A sermon is an urgent message from the living God Himself, a message of which the preacher must see himself as the duly appointed herald. Therefore the preacher must give it all he has. He must not hold back, and he may in no way trifle with his task. God sent him, God gave him the message. So R.B. told his students, "Get on your hind legs and preach!" Though the admonition raises some questions of anatomy, the thrust was clear: "Give it all you've got; don't hold back; you're God's messenger."

A corollary to the preceding was R.B.'s charge to his students that they be fearless in preaching the gospel. Timidity has no place in the pulpit. This advice did not call for an abandonment of all discretion. R.B. knew well and often quoted

Christ's words to His disciples that they be "wise as serpents and harmless a doves" (Mt. 10:16). At the same time he reminded the students of Christ's warning, "Woe to you when all men speak well of you" (Luke 6:26). He also liked to refer to Paul's exhortation to workmen not to labor "as men-pleasers, but in singleness of heart, fearing the Lord" (Col. 3:22). To drive the point home R.B. liked to tell of the two questions that the Methodist John Wesley would regularly put to candidates for the ministry, questions to which he expected an affirmative answer in both instances. The first question was, "Have you made any converts?" and the second was, "Have you made any enemies?" If the candidate did not answer affirmatively in both cases, he was rejected. Of course, R.B. couldn't tell the story without a sly comment on the flaw in a theology that speaks of man's "making converts," since only God by His Spirit can make a convert.

A final item under the heading of important ground rules has to do with R.B.s urging his students to practice and to preach a healthy spirituality. He wanted the seminarians to appreciate their liberal arts education. A spirituality that denigrates the things of nature and culture and history is a false spirituality. Our God is Lord of all of creation and its history, and His salvation encompasses the goal of a new earth as well as a new heaven. He pointed out the large place that natural things had in Christ's teaching in parables. He illustrated his point by referring to an uneducated preacher who boasted that he had not been to college but he had been to Calvary. R.B.'s comment was that though having been to Calvary is of first importance for a preacher, it is highly desirable that the minister of the Word have been to both college and Calvary.

Scriptura Sola—Scriptura Tota

"The Christian preacher must proclaim only the Word of God, and he must declare the whole Word of God."[2] That statement summarizes what was central to all of R.B. Kuiper's teaching on preaching and it is the heart of his chapter on "Scriptural Preaching" in the symposium produced by the Westminster faculty. This is the meaning of the two Latin expressions used in the heading above—Scripture Alone and the Whole Scripture.

Scriptura sola—this and this alone is the ground on which a preacher can and may expect people to listen to him. He is coming with the eternal and faultless wisdom of God, not with the passing and flawed wisdom of men. To cite another Latin phrase that R.B. often used, the preacher is *Verbi Divini Minister*—minister of the divine Word. He is not minister of the human word.

Pushed to its logical conclusion, does this mean that a true sermon must be made up of quotations from Scripture and nothing else? R.B. regarded such comments as sophomoric. The thrust of *Scriptura sola* is that the preacher in all that he says from the pulpit is proclaiming, explaining, illustrating and applying only that which the Bible teaches.

By all means illustrations should be used. And this material is not to be found only in the Bible, though in our age of abysmal ignorance of the contents of the Bible such illustrations are highly recommended. Such material may also be found in general revelation. R.B. referred to the preaching and teaching of none other than Christ Himself. "When Jesus likened the kingdom of heaven to a grain of mustard seed or to leaven, he was, of course, not preaching on mustard seed or leaven, but on the kingdom of God."[3]

May the preacher express himself on current social or political or economic issues? He may and should. Preaching without application is seriously at fault and could be only an academic exercise, which preaching is not. After all, preaching is to people, to people in their historical setting, for their edification, strengthening, comfort and inspiration. In applying the Word to current social problems the preacher does so from the point of view of what the Bible teaches and not from the perspective of the social or political or economic scientist, though he may and should use valid insights they may have to offer. Furthermore, "the Bible is the Word of God for all ages. As such it is ageless . . . The minister should preach the Word, and only the Word. But this does not at all mean that he must ignore the world. It is his business to declare what the Word has to say about the world."[4]

In his insistence on *Scriptura sola* R.B. ruled out certain material as the content of sermons. Preaching must not concentrate on religious experience as its subject matter, though such can be used by way of illustration. The same holds true for the contents of books and biographical data. Book reviews, discussions on the lives of men, and delightful talks on literary themes are not sermons, R.B. insisted. For that matter, R.B. would also assert that essays on theological themes aren't sermons either. On this score he had a word of caution regarding a type of preaching he very much approved of, namely, catechismal preaching. Such preaching must be based on the infallible Word, not on creeds, although a creed can be used as a guide in presenting the biblical teaching. R.B. also had a word of advice for his students regarding the practice of filling sermons with extensive readings from books on theology. He advised against the practice for reasons given above, and because the hearers might go to sleep.

Much the same basic reasoning applies to material that comes under psychology or counselling. R.B. was all in favor of good course material for seminary students in the areas of pastoral psychology or psychiatry and counselling, so that as preachers they might be sensitive to the inner makeup and needs of those who heard them proclaim the Word of truth. But he warned that sermons should not become lectures in psychology or counselling.

R.B. was in dead earnest on the *Scriptura sola* principle. Therefore he never ceased to make plain that "anything but the most painstaking exegesis is unworthy of Christian preaching."[5] His demand for thorough exegesis won the appreciation of the teachers in the departments of Old and New Testament with their stress on mastering the Hebrew and Greek languages. And R.B. was of one mind with his colleagues in his strictures on the views of Karl Barth and dialectical theologians generally in their teaching that the text of Scripure is not the Word of God, but is rather witness to the Word of God. In such views there can, of course, be no talk of preaching the Word of God; that real Word is essentially hidden.

The Whole Bible

In his teaching that the whole Bible (*Scriptura tota*) must be preached, R.B. was not suggesting anything so fatuous as using every verse or passage of Scripture as basis for sermons. Though every passage of Scripture has *historical* authority, every passage does not have *normative* authority as rule for faith and life. The friends of Job, for instance, said what the Bible records as their words to the suffering Job, but not all they said is normative for our lives. Much of what they said had God's disapproval.

The *Scriptura tota* principle does mean, R.B. taught, that the preacher should sermonize on the Old Testament as well as on the New Testament. Neither may be neglected, for the two testaments are an "indissoluble organism" of truth revealing progressively the mind and will of God for the redemption of His people in Christ and their life as His obedient and loving children. But preaching on an Old Testament passage calls for an understanding that goes beyond the Old Testament due to the progressive character of God's revelation. As R.B. put it with his customary succinctness, "A sermon on an Old Testament text must always be a New Testament sermon."[6]

In preaching on the whole Bible the preacher may not fail to do justice to the threefold character of the redemptive message of Christianity. For many years during R.B.'s lifetime a debate was going on concerning the question whether Christianity is a matter of doctrine or of life. This discussion, important as it was, failed to do justice to a third and prior element, namely, that before we can speak of Christian doctrine or Christian life we must stress the Christian story. With Barth's distinction between history and super-history clearly in view, R.B. emphasized that Christian preaching must first of all do justice to the historical character of the Bible's teaching. The modern attack on Scripture has concentrated most heavily on historical aspects of the Bible's teaching, on such specifics as creation, the fall of man, the virgin birth of Christ, the miracles and Christ's resurrection. Only when the preacher does justice to all three—history, doctrine and ethics, can his preaching be called Christian. Only then is he preaching the full gospel.

Because the Bible is an "indissoluble organism" of divine

truth, the preacher may never approach a text and its teaching as if it were an isolated fragment of instruction. The preacher must declare what the apostle Paul called "the whole counsel of God" (Acts 20:17). In other words, the preacher must present the Word of God in full and disciplined awareness of the theology of the Bible. A good preacher must be and is a good theologian. This theological awarenes on the part of the preacher calls for deep appreciation for the teaching of the Christian church in its confessional statements or creeds. The preacher who does his sermonizing solely on his own private interpretation of Scripture in neglect of the Spirit's teaching of Christ's church throughout the centuries is not only depriving himself and his hearers of a rich heritage; he is also guilty of "boundless conceit," according to R.B. Kuiper.[7] To be sure, R.B. knew and taught that a theologically correct discourse is not yet a sermon. But that consideration takes nothing away from the need for thorough theological understanding if there is to be true scriptural preaching. And in the preacher's sensitivity to the theology of the Bible nothing was of more importance to R.B. and his instruction than the Bible's teaching of salvation by the grace of God in all of its rich ramifications. A sermon displaying no awareness of this point was not, in R.B.'s estimation, worthy of being called a sermon.

All of what has been said regarding R.B.'s teaching under the heading of *Scriptura tota* (the whole Bible) can be summarized in two words: Preach Christ. He stands at the center of Scripture. He is the living heartbeat of theology, of all the Bible's teaching. For R.B. there was no conflict between the terms *theocentric preaching* and *christocentric preaching*. They meant the same thing to him, for Christ is God come in the flesh. Furthermore, preaching Christ is not a narrow ministry aiming almost exclusively at the satisfactions of personal salvation. Like his Master before him, the Christian preacher must come proclaiming the Kingdom of God, presenting the claims of Christ in all the rich meaning of that kingship over all of life.

The Ideal Homily

There were some students at Westminster who gave R.B. a problem. These were men who had done considerable "preaching" before they ever came to the seminary. It is probably correct to say that most of these serious-minded students had known very little about disciplined and theologically sensitive study of the Bible. Also, the prior "preaching" of most of them had been done in settings where almost any collection of pious words and phrases sincerely rendered in relation to a passage of Scripture was called a sermon. Such students confronted R.B. with the task of getting them to unlearn a lot of notions about preaching they had entertained and practiced as well as to get across to them just what good preaching is. R.B.'s problem with such students became apparent one day as a seminarian was busy in the library reading commentaries in preparing a sermon. He was working on his second or third sermon required in R.B.'s class in Homiletics. He had delivered a sermon in class which clearly had left much to be desired. As this student was busy with the books he raised his head and said to us who were reading nearby, "These commentaries sure do help, don't they." His remark left the distinct impression that he had not consulted them before.

But R.B. was patient with such students as well as with the rest of us. We all had a lot to learn. His patience could wear thin if he felt that a student had not really worked on his sermon and was trying to get away with bluffing it. Then the professor's critique could be sharp.

R.B. taught his students that all preaching must be expository, that is, exposition of the Scriptures. "Exposition of Scipture, exposition worthy of the name, is of the very essence of preaching. It follows that it is a serious error to recommend expository preaching as one of several legitimate methods. Nor is it at all satisfactory, after the manner of many conservatives, to extol the expository method as the best. All preaching must be expository. Only expository preaching can be Scriptural."[8] In speaking thus R.B. was expressing his objection to allegorical preaching, a style often practiced under the notion that it gets at the deeper spiritual meaning of a passage of Scripture. As a matter of fact such preaching often does great violence to Scripture, according to R.B. And he was also objecting to the commonly held opinion that only a running commentary on an extended portion of Scripture (a chapter, perhaps) could be called expository preaching.

The running commentary type of preaching has certain glaring faults, according to Kuiper. The exegesis tends to be superficial, since so much material has to be covered. And such sermons often lack unity, so that the hearer has no clear idea as to just what the sermon is about. Such sermons may excel in analysis of text, but they lack synthesis with the rest of the teaching of Scripture and thus do violence to the *Scriptura tota* principle. Good preaching compares Scripture with Scripture in order that the correct and full teaching of the Bible on a subject may be conveyed.

The ideal homily,[9] R.B. taught, is a combination of analysis and synthesis. In this method of sermon construction the text is thoroughly analyzed (exegesis) and it is related to the teaching of the Bible as a whole on the subject being preached about (synthesis). This method can and should be used whether the text is longer or shorter. The preacher must delve diligently into the text to determine what is the main idea of the passage. That then becomes the theme of the sermon, and it can be phrased so as to attract the attention of the hearers. Under that theme a number of main points (two, three, four or even five) of about equal significance are listed as exhausting the teaching of the text. The whole structure (theme, main points with sub-points, together with illustrations from Scripture and life, and application) then forms an orderly and logical discourse that altogether drives home what the Word of the living God has to say in its saving power.

An illustration of this method of sermon preparation as presented by R.B. is the following essential outline for a sermon on John 3:16. The theme of the sermon is *The Greatness of God's Love*. Under this heading are three main thoughts, as follows: (I) The object of His love (the world); (II) The gift of His love (His only begotten Son); (III) The purpose of His love (the salvation of believers). It is obvious that such preaching calls for a lot of study and reflection as the preacher uncovers the central theme of a passage of Scripture and then develops that teaching in an orderly manner.

R.B. did not for one moment claim, nor is it suggested here, that this instruction on the ideal homily was original with him. But there was something that gave the teaching of this professor of Homiletics special relevance and force. That something was R.B.'s own preaching. He not only taught this method of sermonizing; he practiced it, brilliantly and powerfully. "What a great but rare gift this is for one who teaches young men to preach!" Professor Klooster of Calvin Seminary wrote those apt words as part of his tribute to Kuiper's preaching.[10] R.B. could present the ideal homily not just as a professor's pet scheme, but as an important, visible factor in the marked success of a great preacher. This is the best way to preach the Word, R.B. taught. And when he preached, his hearers knew he preached the Word most effectively. It would be hard to find a person, even a fairly young child, who, after hearing R.B. Kuiper preach, had any uncertainty as to what the minister had been talking about.

With regard to this method of preaching one item deserves emphasis. It has to do with the ministry of logic, of orderly thinking. Diffuseness is the enemy of good discourse and is also the enemy of edification. Much preaching suffers from diffuseness. The thoughts of the preacher are often not sharply focussed. They are spread thin and helter-skelter over a broad and ill-defined range. The method of preaching R.B. sought to teach his students called for earnest, disciplined and orderly thought. One of Westminster's better students wrote as follows to Professor Kuiper when he retired in 1952, "I think that of all my professors your influence did more for me than that of any of the others." When at a later date he was asked just what he meant he replied that R.B. Kuiper taught him the meaning and value of orderly thinking, of logic, and he was deeply grateful for that instruction; it had been of immense worth to him in his ministry of preaching and teaching.

The Importance of Practical Theology

Professor Kuiper as incumbent in the chair of Practical Theology pursued his task as one who believed he had an important work to do. Working with the principle that Practical Theology is theology, he expanded his teaching well beyond instruction in the science and art of preaching (Homiletics). His course offerings expanded until they covered every phase of the work of the pastor. Other basic courses were in Church Government and Public Worship (Liturgics). He also taught courses in Doctrinal Preaching, Ethical Preaching, History of Preaching, Environmental Evangelism, Missions (often taught in whole or in part by some one with missionary experience), Pastoral Care (Poimenics) and Covenant Implications. In the last named course R.B. taught his students (coming from many different backgrounds) to see the need and the Christian rationale for an agency of which he had always been a strong champion, namely, the Christian day school.

At an event at which members of the faculty, students and some close friends of the seminary were gathered Dr. Machen gave a brief talk on what constitutes a theological seminary. Of highest importance, he declared, is a properly equipped faculty. There could conceivably be a seminary without buildings or students, but there could not be one without a suitable faculty. He then gave his ideas on what such a faculty is and what it seeks to do. He spoke appreciatively of the contribution of each department of Westminster Seminary. The last department he spoke about was that of Practical Theology, which he said was in some ways the most important one because it sought to apply all that the students had learned at the seminary to the actual work of ministering in the Word. His remarks took on added warmth as he spoke of Professor Kuiper's work. Obviously Dr. Machen felt that the department of Practical Theology was doing the work it was set up to do, and it was doing that work very well.

Chapter 15

The Presbyterian Churchman

He served in three different denominations in his lifetime. Up to now he had served in the Christian Reformed Church in North America and the Reformed Church in America. In February of 1937 he became a Presbyterian Churchman. At that time he was received as a member of the Presbytery of Philadelphia of the Presbyterian Church of America,[1] a church which changed its name to the Orthodox Presbyterian Church just two years later.

R.B.'s membership in the Orthodox Presbyterian Church was in part a response to the urging of his dear friend and associate Dr. J. Gresham Machen. In the last conversation Machen had with Kuiper prior to his death on January 1, 1937, he urged R.B. to join the new church. Association with the church had been on R.B.'s mind for some time, and the last wish of his beloved colleague pushed him to make the decision to leave the Christian Reformed Church a second time. Dr. C. Van Til joined the new movement shortly before Kuiper did.

The Presbyterian Church of America, hereinafter called by its more familiar name the Orthodox Presbyterian Church (except where the original name appears in quotations), came into existence in 1936. The occasion was a sharp conflict over the way in which the Presbyterian Church in the U.S.A. (then also known as the large "northern" Presbyterian Church) carried on the main business of the church, that of evangelizing the world. For some years criticism had been leveled at the denominational Board of Foreign Missions over policies and practices that allegedly compromised the biblical and confessional stance of the church.

In the early thirties the conflict over foreign missions reached crisis stage mainly because of two developments. The first of these came in 1932 with the publication of the book *Re-Thinking Missions*. The second factor aggravating the unrest was the published views of the noted missionary author Pearl S. Buck, whose best known work is the novel *The Good Earth*. In a widely-read magazine the Presbyterian missionary wrote as follows, "To some of us He is still the divine Son of God, born of the Virgin Mary, conceived by the Holy Spirit. But to many of us He has ceased to be that." "I do not believe in original sin." "I agree with the Chinese who feel their people should be protected from such superstition" (meaning teaching about salvation from sin).[2] Of the book *Re-Thinking Missions* Mrs. Buck wrote that it "presents a masterly statement of religion in its place in life, and of Christianity in its place in religion."[3]

It was these developments that caused Machen to feel that he had to speak his mind. He prepared a document of more than a hundred pages on "Modernism and the Board of Foreign Missions of the Presbyterian Church in the U.S.A." In this extended pamphlet he called the book *Re-Thinking Missions* "an attack against the very heart of the Christian religion." He dealt with the views of Pearl S. Buck and other Presbyterian missionaries. The growing clamor in the church and outside it forced the Board to ask Mrs. Buck to appear before it. She refused and resigned. The Board accepted her resignation "with regret." Also the Board refused to take a clear-cut stand on the book *Re-Thinking Missions*, a volume in whose preparation the Presbyterian Church in the U.S.A. had been involved through a representative who was a signer of the Auburn Affirmation.

A New Mission Board

The whole matter of the Board's performance came before the General Assembly. The action taken by the Assembly did not satisfy the conservatives in the church. The result was the formation of a new agency for carrying on the church's foreign mission work. It was called the Independent Board for Presbyterian Foreign Missions. Dr. Machen was elected president. Due in good part to the labors of an able and winsome General

Secretary (Rev. Charles J. Woodbridge, former missionary to Africa) the new agency quickly attracted sympathizers, money and missionaries to serve under it.

Official action against the new board came quickly. In 1934 the General Assembly demanded that the Independent Board cease functioning and that its members resign. The Assembly also took the remarkable position that a congregation or church member is under obligation to support the official missionary program of the church in the same way that he is under obligation to partake of the Lord's Supper. Dr. Clarence Macartney, prominent Presbyterian pastor in Pittsburg and not a member of the Independent Board, was outraged at this deliverance of the General Assembly. He declared that the Assembly "erred grievously, deeply and dangerously," and condemned the action as being "in its spirit and tone harsh, severe, unscriptural and un-Presbyterian . . . unjust and unconstitutional . . . unspeakable." He wrote further that the action "savors more of a papal bull than of the deliberations of the General Assembly of a free Protestant Church."[4]

Dr. Machen and his associates on the Independent Board refused to bow to the demands of the General Assembly. Consequently these people were brought to trial before the courts of the church in their various presbyteries. The most dramatic and publicized of the trials was that of J. Gresham Machen before a Judicial Commission of the Presbytery of New Brunswick in New Jersey. The chairman of the Commission was a signer of the Auburn Affirmation.

R.B. Kuiper witnessed most of the trial of Dr. Machen. He was especially incensed at the presence on the judicial panel of Dr. John E. Kuizenga, former editor of *The Leader*, publication of the Reformed Church in America, whose writings R.B. had once read with appreciation. Kuizenga had been appointed to the Chair of Apologetics at Princeton Seminary after J.G. Machen's appointment to the Chair had been sidetracked at the General Assembly by his enemies. Regarding the trial R.B. wrote that it "affords a striking revelation of the destructive influence of liberalism and liberal leanings on Christian ethics." He felt that Machen didn't get even a semblance of a fair deal in that the ecclesiastical court deliberately destroyed his defense beforehand by denying him any chance to explain why the Independent Board was established and why he could not obey the mandate of the General Assembly.[5]

The outcome of Machen's trial was a foregone conclusion. With the issue reduced to the simple question of his obedience or disobedience before the mandate of the General Assembly, the Judicial Commission had little trouble finding him guilty and worthy of suspension from the ministry of the Presbyterian Church in the U.S.A. As could also have been foreseen, all ensuing appeals failed.

The New Church

With Machen and at least seven other clergymen suspended, the formation of a new church was now inevitable. It was born on June 11, 1936, and its stated intent was "to continue what we believe to be the true spiritual succession of the Presbyterian Church in the U.S.A., which we hold to have been abandoned by the present organization of that body."[6] The new organization chose as its name the Presbyterian Church of America and Dr. Machen was elected Moderator of the organizing Assembly. "A True Presbyterian Church at Last" was the title of an article appearing in a new magazine named *The Presbyterian Guardian*. The article, written by Machen, contained a significant confession: "What a fearful sin of omission it was . . . that an effort was not made in 1924, in every single Presbytery in which any of us stood, to bring the Auburn Affirmationists to trial!" R.B. often said that this failure was the biggest single mistake of those seeking reform in the Presbyterian Church in the U.S.A. Machen's article spoke of the gathering of the new church at its first assembly as follows, "What a joyous moment it was! How the long years of struggle seemed to sink into nothingness compared with the peace and joy that filled our hearts."[7]

R.B. entertained no doubts as to the legitimacy of the founding of the new church. Others did have such doubts. Able men like Westminster Professor O.T. Allis and Rev. Clarence Macartney of the Board of Trustees did not go along with the new movement and resigned their positions at Westminster Seminary, to the great regret of Machen and his colleagues.

Though Westminster as an independent school was not officially bound to any church, the flow of events at the time plus the active involvement of the faculty members in the new church made these men feel they had to break with the seminary. Allis and Macartney with others felt that they should remain in the Presbyterian Church in the U.S.A. as long as it officially held to its historic creeds, and that their duty was to work for reform from within.

Kuiper came down hard and strong on this issue. He declared that those who founded the new church not only had a right to do so, "they had to do it. It was their solemn duty." He asserted that those who would remain to seek reform from within were "pussyfooting." In fact, he said emphatically they were "sinning." They were abetting the false witness of a denomination that had become "flagrantly disloyal to the faith of the fathers."[8] With respect to those who felt that they could stay in the old church as long as that body did not alter its official statements of faith, its creeds, R.B. often said that the liberals don't think enough of their creeds to bother with changing them. He also observed that church politicians know that when you start tampering with the creeds of the church, troublesome questions arise in the minds of the plain folk in the church.

Being fully persuaded that the formation of the new church was in no way schismatic, R.B. had no hesitation in joining it. Nor did the Christian Reformed Church regard the new Presbyterian church as schismatic. It was the first ecclesiastical body to give official recognition to the new church. The Synod of the Christian Reformed Church wired its best wishes to the new organization and asked them to appoint a fraternal delegate. Of significance in the Synod's message was the acknowledgement of "the tie that binds us in the propagation and defense of our common Reformed faith."

Peace Short-lived

The peace that Machen hailed at the first Assembly of the new church did not last long. The resignations of Allis, Macartney and others at Westminster were deeply disturbing. Other troublesome developments arose out of the fact that not all those who stood united in their opposition to modernism were of one mind in their allegiance to the Reformed faith.

In his article on "The Presbyterian Church of America" in *The Banner* R.B. had expressed himself as follows in speaking of the First General Assembly, "The General Assembly had the privilege of examining several graduates of Westminster Seminary for licensure and ordination. It would have warmed the cockles of the heart of any Christian Reformed minister to hear how closely they were questioned about the two errors which are so extremely prevalent among American fundamentalists, Arminianism and the Dispensationalism of the Scofield Bible. The Assembly wanted to make sure that their prospective ministers were not tainted with such anti-reformed heresies."

To R.B.'s amazement these words provoked a storm. At the center of the storm was Rev. Cal McIntire, New Jersey minister in the Orthodox Presbyterian Church. In a paper of which he was editor and publisher named *Christian Beacon* he wrote an editorial in which he charged that Kuiper in his remarks about the Dispensationalism of the Scofield Bible had called premillennialists heretics. McIntire, an avowed premillennialist, refused to publish a letter from R.B. Kuiper in answer to the charge. The extended correspondence R.B. had with McIntire in an effort to clarify the matter proved to be an exercise in futility.

The issue came to a head at the Second General Assembly of the church, held in November of 1936. Dr. James O. Buswell, Jr., president of Wheaton College in Illinois, was elected moderator of the assembly. He was also an outspoken premillennialist, and his election plainly demonstrated that there was freedom in the church in one's convictions regarding the events connected with Christ's second coming. In the debates on the issue it was interesting to hear Buswell speak of amillennialism as a "heresy." Strenuous efforts were put forth to have the Assembly make some kind of declaration that would indicate that the church did not interpret its confessional standards as being at any point opposed to the premillennial point of view. All such proposals were rejected on the ground that liberty in such matters did already exist within the bounds of the constitution of the church.

Of greater significance was an action that demonstrated

how intent the new church was on being uncompromisingly Reformed. The second Assembly adopted the confessional standards of the church. Discussions had been going on in print and elsewhere with regard to certain amendments to the Westminster Confession adopted by the Presbyterian Church in the U.S.A. in 1903. Able theologians like Professors John Murray and Machen contended that these amendments compromised the Reformed stance of the Confession, a compromise adopted in order that merger with a smaller Presbyterian body with strong Arminian leanings could be achieved. The second Assembly of the Orthodox Presbyterian Church dropped these amendments in adopting the Westminster Confession and Catechisms as its doctrinal standards. R.B. Kuiper heartily applauded the action. But there was a minority in the church which opposed dropping the 1903 amendments.

Another sharp difference of opinion broke out in the fledgling church over the matter of Christian liberty in the use of alcoholic beverages. There were those, notably McIntire and Buswell, who maintained that the only proper Christian practice is that of total abstinence and the church should so declare. Overtures to that effect came to the Third General Assembly. Even though the large majority of the delegates to the Assembly were total abstainers, these overtures were overwhelmingly rejected on the ground that the Bible is our only and adequate rule in these questions of morals, and a study of the Bible together with the subordinate standards (Westminster Confession and Catechisms) gives the necessary guidance in such matters; no more rules are needed, especially when such rules go beyond what the Bible teaches.

Still another issue disturbed the peace of the young church. This had to do with the relationship of the new church to the very agency that had been the center of dispute with the Presbyterian Church in the U.S.A., namely, the Independent Board for Presbyterian Foreign Missions. Machen and others very definitely expected the Board to be an agency for Presbyterian missions, that is, missions loyal to the Reformed faith and Presbyterian church government. But there were a number on the Board who thought otherwise, some even promoting independency in church polity. The seriousness of this difference of opinion surfaced in a meeting of the Independent

Board in November of 1936, shortly after the Second General Assembly. At this meeting Dr. Machen was voted out of the chairmanship of the Board, a position he had held from the beginning. Machen took this as a serious blow, not to his pride, but to his hopes for the continuing Reformed witness of the program of missions under the Board's direction. R.B. reported that in his first personal encounter with Machen after his ouster from the presidency he said, "Kuiper, the Independent Board is lost for the cause of the Reformed faith." At the next General Assembly the new church broke its ties with the Independent Board and proceeded to carry out its foreign missions program under its own Committee on Foreign Missions.

It is noteworthy that those in the church who opposed dropping the 1903 amendments, who pushed for more elbow room for premillennialism, who called for a ruling favoring total abstinence, and who opposed severing the church's connection with the Independent Board were in the main the same minority in the church. And when this minority was frustrated at every turn, the group decided to leave the Orthodox Presbyterian Church and to form a new body called the Bible Presbyterian Synod. It was at this time that Dr. A.A. MacRae left the faculty of Westminster Seminary. One of the first actions of the new organization was to amend the Westminster Confession and Catechisms so that they clearly expressed the premillennial point of view.

So in less than a year after the break with the Presbyterian Church in the U.S.A. the Orthodox Presbyterian Church experienced a split. Not a very pretty picture, one affording no little satisfaction to the group's detractors. This sad spectacle drew a pointed commentary from R.B. In speaking of the parties at loggerheads in the Orthodox Presbyterian Church he said, "The church might easily have been held together. To do so would have required no special wisdom. If the church had only done what most churches are doing right along, there would have been no thought of a split. The path of least resistance is to place peace over purity. Had it been followed, the Presbyterian Church of America would have saved its face. As a matter of fact, the Third General Assembly presented a spectacle so unusual that few seem able to comprehend. Here actually was a church at work which would rather be small than wrong, which

preferred disrepute to compromise."[9] R.B. had joined the
church in February prior to the meeting of the Third General
Assembly in the late spring of 1937.

A Busy Churchman

R.B. Kuiper's gifts and experience were soon put to good
use in the Orthodox Presbyterian Church. At the very first
General Assembly he attended as a member of the church he was
chosen to serve on the standing Committee on Foreign Missions.
The Third General Assembly also elected him to a committee on
the constitution of the church, with a mandate to work on the
Book of Discipline and the Directory for the Public Worship of
God. At the same Assembly he delivered a memorial address on
"Dr. Machen as a Reformer."

Thus R.B. got to work at once to do his part to rebuild and
strengthen the fractured church. In 1938 he was elected
Moderator of the Fourth General Assembly. He served on many
committees. In the book about the denomination entitled *The
First Ten Years* R.B. is listed in a group of ten men described as
having been most active in committee work in the second half of
the first decade of the church's life. Besides serving on two of
the three standing committees of the church (Foreign Missions
and then Home Missions), he was active on many special committees, some of them of crucial importance in the life of the
church. His seasoned wisdom, mature judgment, ingratiating
wit and the unerring relevance of his observations were a stabiliz-
ing force. And he was highly astute in assessing the political
dynamics at work in the councils of the church.

The Christian and lodge membership, the church's responsibility in theological education, a new hymnal, the use of
psalms and/or hymns in public worship, the ecumenical responsibilities of the church—these were some of the more important
committee projects on which R.B. served the Orthodox
Presbyterian Church. A concrete result of these labors was the
appearance of a booklet entitled *Christ or the Lodge*, of which
R.B. was the main author. Another concrete result came much
later in the publication of the *Trinity Hymnal* in 1961. Though
this date is long after R.B.'s departure from the Orthodox

Presbyterian Church in 1953, he was much involved in the formulation of the principles that governed the choices of the 730 songs in this widely used book of praise.

Theological Education—Whose Job?

There were problems in the Orthodox Presbyterian Church in the thirties, we have seen. Another period of unrest and tension came in the mid-forties. There were those in the church who became dissatisfied with what they felt was too slow a rate of growth. This dissatisfaction was directed in large part at the leadership role of the faculty of Westminster Seminary in the church. An overture came to the Eleventh General Assembly in 1944 requesting that steps be taken to seek church control of the seminary. This request launched a debate on who is responsible for the theological education of the future ministers of the church. A committee of five was chosen to study the question. Professors Kuiper, Murray and Woolley of Westminster Seminary served on this committee, and they brought a majority report which concluded with this judgment, "The commission given by God to His church requires the conduct on the part of the church of certain forms of theological education. There are, however, strict limits to the scope of the theological education that may properly be undertaken by the church . . . Since the church must not exceed the terms of its commission and must limit itself to those activities which Holy Scripture establishes as the proper function of the church, it is the judgment of the Committee that it would be a usurpation of authority and a violation of the order which Christ has instituted in His church for the church to undertake the comprehensive theological education which is ordinarily and properly undertaken by theological seminaries or by theological faculties in universities."[10]

Each of the professors added a separate monograph in support of this conclusion. In his contribution R.B. argued that "prospective ministers of the gospel must be taught theology as a science; and, since science operates both in the sphere of nature and in that of sovereign grace, it must be taught, not by the state, which belongs to the sphere of nature, nor by the church, which belongs to the sphere of saving grace, but by the

Christian family, which belongs to both."[11] A minority report brought by two pastors held that a church "certainly *may* conduct theological education for the training of the ministry," but it is not in principle bound to do so. Therefore the minority recommended that a committee on theological education be erected for the purpose of maintaining "effective contact" with Westminster Seminary.

The Assembly took no action on the question of theological education but turned it over to a new committee of five on which there was only one Westminster faculty member (Stonehouse). This new committee, in speaking of the majority and minority reports brought to the previous Assembly, declared that "both reports are in fundamental agreement on one basic point, viz., the judgment that it is not necessary, *as a matter of principle*, for the church to provide comprehensive theological education for the training of its ministerial candidates. This conclusion is of the greatest possible significance. While it may be challenged in certain quarters, we do not challenge it."[12]

Another point of agitation in the Orthodox Presbyterian Church in the mid-forties was the demand for closer relations with other Christian groups, especially with the American Council of Christian Churches, an organization in which Rev. Carl McIntire was a dominating figure. R.B. served on a committee to study possible membership in the American Council and the Scriptural principles of cooperation with other Christian churches. Those interested in ecumenism from a biblical perspective should find the report of this committee worthwhile reading.[13] It clearly bears the mark of R.B. Kuiper's writing. A majority of the committee recommended constituent membership in the Council. A minority of Kuiper and Stonehouse recommended "no action" on joining either the American Council of Christian Churches or the National Association of Evangelicals. They saw membership in either organization as impairing the church's Calvinistic witness. The Assembly decided to appoint a small committee to pursue the possibility of a "consultative relationship" with the American Council. There is no evidence that such a relationship ever materialized.

A Difficult Case

Neither R.B. Kuiper in his rich and full career nor the Orthodox Presbyterian Church ever faced a more complex or difficult issue than that turning around the ordination of ruling elder Dr. Gordon H. Clark as a minister of the gospel. Dr. Clark was a man of considerable intellectual strength. He had been a stalwart figure in the Orthodox Presbyterian Church from its very beginning. He was a professor of Philosophy, and while teaching at Wheaton College he had introduced a number of prospective students at Westminster Seminary to the Reformed faith. A movement developed to seek his ordination to the gospel ministry. Part of the reason for seeking his ordination was that it was seen by the dissatisfied group in the church in the mid-forties as a stratagem by which to achieve some of the goals that this group pursued.

The debate over Dr. Clark's views was a protracted and complicated affair. Unfortunately it involved a man who had rendered commendable service in the church, a fact that made opposition to his views an unpleasant exercise. And the points at issue lay at the deeper levels of Christian thought, points such as the incomprehensibility of God, the primacy of the intellect, the influence of regeneration on man's intellectual activity, the relation between divine sovereignty and human responsibility, and the free offer of the gospel to all people. During the protracted discussions on the complex theological issues involved one minister sighed that he hoped the church would never again have to examine a professional philosopher. R.B. Kuiper was one of the first to enter a protest against the actions of the Presbytery of Philadelphia at a special meeting of that body in July of 1944, a meeting at which Dr. Clark was examined for licensure, his examination sustained, and a decision taken to proceed to his ordination at a future date agreed upon. The church was thoroughly stirred over this issue. Many words were written and spoken. The General Assembly of 1946, responding to a complaint against the actions of the Presbytery of Philadelphia, found that the Presbytery had erred in finding the examination for licensure adequate for ordination and in immediately deciding to ordain Dr. Clark at a set future date. But the

Assembly did not find the Presbytery in error in sustaining Clark's examination. Against this failure of the Assembly forty-three commissioners entered a protest read by John Murray, professor of Systematic Theology at Westminster Seminary. Most, if not all, of the other professors at the seminary also signed the protest. The first ground of the protest stated that Dr. Clark had not given "satifactory answers respecting important questions of doctrine."[14] The Assembly appointed a committee to give further study to the doctrinal issues in the case.[15]

The frustrations that the dissatisfied group in the church had experienced in the failure to gain church control of Westminster Seminary, the failure to gain constituent membership in the American Council of Christian Churches, and the rebuke suffered in the ordination of Dr. Clark came to a head at the Fourteenth General Assembly meeting at Cedar Grove, Wisconsin, in 1947. The group seeking these objectives lost a crucial standing committee election by just one vote. After this critical vote had been taken several commissioners arose to announce their resignation from standing committees of the church. These resignations were followed by the departure of several ministers and elders from the church, including Rev. Clark.

R.B. Kuiper in Geneva

Geneva in Switzerland—what a name for one so immersed in Reformation teaching as R.B. Kuiper was. In the summer of 1950 Professor and Mrs. R.B. Kuiper were in this celebrated city made famous by the labors of that prince of theologians, John Calvin, in the sixteenth century. It was more than his sense of history that stirred R.B. as he moved about in Geneva. It was his sense of the truth that he embraced so wholeheartedly that excited his soul as he walked the short and narrow Rue Jean Calvin, and stood at the point where a plaque marked the place where the great Reformer had lectured for many years.

It was at the International Monument to the Reformation that the souls of the two visitors were most affected. R.B., unabashed and articulate Calvinist that he was, was stirred on seeing this impressively eloquent monument to the faith that had captured his heart and the hearts of millions more. The monument takes the form of a wall more than three hundred feet long and about twenty-five feet high. Ten large statues sculpted in the stone of the wall tell the story of a spiritual-intellectual impulse that gave a new vision of life under the motto engraved in the wall in large letters—POST TENEBRAS LUX (after darkness light), the light being the true understanding of the Word of Truth, the Bible. The eyes of Rev. and Mrs. Kuiper were fixed especially on the cluster of four tall statues that form the centerpiece of the monument. These are the statues of Farel, Calvin, Beza and Knox. These four Reformers were together in Geneva in 1559 when the Geneva Academy was founded. Calvin stands a half-step ahead of the other three, indicating he was the leader of this movement that so profoundly affected not only the church, but governments and societies as well. At the ends of the monument and just across the water-filled moat before the wall are huge blocks of stone with the name of Luther engraved in the one and the name of Zwingli in the other.

The Kuipers were slow in leaving the Reformation memorial with its heroic proportions, its fascinating statues, its bas-reliefs, its engraved citations (also from the Mayflower Compact), and "Les Bastions" (the strongholds), the appropriately named park and gardens fronting the wall and moat. But R.B. was not in Geneva as a tourist. He was there on business. He and Dr. N.B. Stonehouse were there as official delegates to the Second Plenary Congress of the International Council of Christian Churches.

As delegate to the Congress Kuiper and Stonehouse were obligated to press for certain changes in the constitution of the International Council that the Orthodox Presbyterian Church was proposing. These proposed changes were aimed at having the Council make clear in its constitution that it did not and would not engage in activities that are properly the task of the church and not of a council of churches, with evangelism especially in view. In the debates on the matter R.B. spoke as follows, according to his report on the Congress to the General Assembly, "Much emphasis has been placed in the sessions of this Congress on those doctrines on which the various churches here represented are in substantial agreement. While that is easily understandable and altogether proper, it may not be forgotten that there are important doctrinal differences among us. Think, for instance, of the difference between the Reformed faith and Arminianism. Because these differences affect in a direct way the preaching of the gospel, the International Council should not engage in evangelism. As a Calvinist I would not wish to be held responsible for what I consider to be Arminian errors, and I imagine my Arminian brethren would not consent to become responsible for my distinctively Calvinistic presentation of the gospel. There are indeed wide areas in which the churches constituting the Council can cooperate, but evangelism is not one of them." At one point in the lively discussions on the matter Rev. Carl McIntire, President of the International Council, declared that if the Orthodox Presbyterian Church persisted in pressing this issue he would rather have that body sever its ties with the Council. R.B.'s report stated that "my stay at Geneva was not all pleasure," though he did say that he enjoyed many aspects of the Congress with its "exhilarating atmosphere of ecumenicity."

A major item on R.B.'s agenda at the Geneva Congress was the delivery of an address on the subject "The Atonement According to the Bible." Also with this speech R.B. managed to provoke discussion. He simply could not fail to be Reformed, particularly not when speaking on such a subject in the city of John Calvin. In his report to the home church he said, "Perhaps

R.B. speaking in Geneva with Dr. Carl McIntire on the right.

I may be pardoned for saying that I aimed to make this address distinctively Reformed, and that it was well received. A brother who certainly does not rate as a rock-ribbed Calvinist paid me the somewhat dubious compliment that he agreed with almost all I said. While it goes without saying that not nearly all the addresses delivered and the resolutions adopted were distinctively Reformed, and while occasionally un-Reformed views came momentarily to expression, there was an almost complete avoidance of theological matters on which evangelical churches are commonly known to differ. This was as might be expected. Yet the undersigned adhered to no such policy. It is his firm conviction, to which he sought to adhere particularly in his address, that the witness of the Orthodox Presbyterian Church may never be less than Reformed.''[16]

The Kuipers' visit to the lovely city on Lake Geneva with its sapphire waters was followed by a time of sight-seeing in Europe and in the British Isles. A number of friendships were renewed with individuals who had visited or lectured at Westminster Seminary. A high point in the European travels was a visit to R.B.'s birthplace in Garrelsweer in the province of Groningen, The Netherlands.

Farewell to the Orthodox Presbyterian Church

His report to the Eighteenth General Assembly (1951) on the visit to Geneva was R.B.'s last significant contribution to the work and life of the Orthodox Presbyterian Church. This was the last General Assembly he attended. A year later he retired from the faculty of Westminster Theological Seminary and left the Philadelphia area to return to Grand Rapids. Fifteen action-packed and productive years in the Orthodox Presbyterian Church came to an end. He had done his part to help guide the little ship through the choppy-to-rough waters of American church life on a journey that any church strongly devoted to the historic Reformed faith would find plagued with problems. The church grew steadily but slowly in those years. That fact, surprising as it may sound to some, was quite in keeping with Machen's hopes for the new church. He had indicated to several of his associates, Kuiper among them, that he did not care to see the new church grow too rapidly. He wanted people coming into the church to understand clearly that it took its Calvinistic confession seriously.

R.B.'s contributions to the church were deeply appreciated. This chapter can best be brought to a close by a quotation from a letter written to R.B. at the time of his official dismissal to the Christian Reformed Church. The letter was written by Rev. John P. Galbraith, for many years a leader in the Orthodox Presbyterian Church. Galbraith wrote as follows, "For so many years you were a tremendously steadying and constructive influence in the OPC in a time when you were sorely needed, and I think that the Church is, as it should be, immensely grateful for the work you have done among us. I know that I, personally, feel that it was your influence more than that of any one individual that served to point us in the right direction. I had hoped that after your retirement you were going to be active still in the Church, for we still need you very much. However, that is not to be, but I want you to know how much many of us wish it were.''

Chapter 16

President of Calvin Seminary

Back to Grand Rapids—this was the move Rev. and Mrs. R.B. Kuiper made in the summer of 1952. This center of Reformed church life held strong attraction for them. Returning there was a kind of homecoming for the Kuipers. He had pastored three churches here at a time when his power and popularity as a preacher had been at their peak. So they still had many friends here. Here were Calvin College and Seminary, institutions which had filled such a prominent place in the family from which R.B. came. And, of course, he had been president of Calvin College. Furthermore, R.B. wanted to continue to be an active churchman and writer. For this reason too he settled in this center of Reformed life and learning.

The Kuipers quickly reestablished ties with the congregation where they had had their happiest years, the Sherman Street Christian Reformed Church. They made this their church home. But it is interesting to note that R.B. did not sever his official ties with the Orthodox Presbyterian Church until more than a year after they returned to Grand Rapids. In October of 1953 he severed his connections with the Presbytery of Philadelphia and became Associate Pastor of the Sherman Street Church. It seems that he was a bit reluctant to leave the fellowship of a church where he had labored so long and so hard to help establish a genuinely Reformed witness on the uneven turf of American protestantism.

Of no small personal importance was the presence of family. Daughter Marietta lived in Grand Rapids with her husband and four children. It was a happy time for all when R.B. and Mrs. Kuiper came to live nearby. Son Klaudius and his family had enjoyed the company of Pa and Ma Kuiper for many years in Philadelphia. Now it was the privilege of the other family to have that pleasure. Many times of happy family togetherness lay ahead.

The four grandchildren were delighted to have the company of Bop and Mom, the names they had attached to these grandparents. No children ever had a grandfather who was a better storyteller than R.B. The Kuipers would hardly be inside the door to our home and one or two of the children would be pulling at R.B.'s sleeve to draw him to the sofa so that he could sit down with them and tell a story. He never disappointed them. Often the story came from the Bible, favorites being of Daniel in the lion's den (they loved to hear Bop roar like a lion) or of Peter's escape from prison. Or the story might be something of R.B.'s own invention. A delightful bit of nonsense came to my ears one day as R.B. was entertaining the children. "Ouch!" cried the elephant.

"What's the matter?" asked Mrs. Elephant.

"My foot hurts."

"How did that happen?"

"A mouse stepped on my toe."

Whatever the story, it was told with exuberant drama. When these exciting storytelling sessions came shortly before bedtime, we often wondered how readily the children would fall asleep after being regaled in such stirring fashion by their grandfather.

Retirement Deferred

He had retired from Westminster, not first of all to enjoy days of relaxation and fun with loved ones, but rather to produce writings that would enhance the witness to the Reformed faith on a broad popular front. His years of study, reflection and teaching were ready to bear fruit in books. But this goal had to be deferred. What happened was in some ways a repeat of what had taken place in 1930. Then R.B.'s plan to return to the pastorate was sidetracked by a call from the Christian Reformed Church to special service as president of Calvin College. Now in 1952 the Christian Reformed Church was calling him to special service again, this time to what would be the presidency of Calvin Seminary. The Synod of 1952, meeting in June, appointed him to teach Practical Theology at the seminary. His name had not been on the original nomination made by the Board of Trustees. But when it became known that R.B. Kuiper was retiring from Westminster and was planning to return to Grand Rapids, the Synod added his name to the nomination and he was elected.

Seminary in Turmoil

The situation at Calvin Seminary was at the time a most extraordinary one, so extraordinary that R.B. felt compelled to accept the appointment and to delay his planned retirement. In fact, the state of affairs at the school had become such that it was labelled the "Seminary Situation." Several overtures came to the Synod asking that corrective action be taken with regard to the "Seminary Situation."

The gravity of the problem was highlighted by the remarks by which the Reporter of the Synod's Advisory Committee on Seminary matters introduced the report of the committee on the floor of synod. "This is a solemn hour!" declared the Reporter. "This is a day of humiliation! All of us are conscious of the weight of the issue which shall now engage our earnest attention . . . It is enough to make one weep."[1] In their statement of the problem the Advisory Committee through its Reporter indicated that the situation had been building for some years, and had grown to such proportions that now "drastic disciplinary measures" had to be recommended. The Synod of 1951 had appointed a committee of seven to "thoroughly investigate all matters in connection with the Seminary Situation with particular reference to appointments."[2]

The Advisory Committee judged that the problem was "first of all one of intra-faculty relations . . . a violent clash between men." There is no hard evidence that the church took note of any doctrinal differences in this highly charged set of circumstances. Basing their findings and recommendations mainly on the report of the Investigation Committee, Synod's Advisory Committee came with drastic proposals. The committee recommended that two professors not be reappointed, that the "tenure of office" of two others be terminated, and that a fifth professor be dismissed. After days of intense deliberation, with the faculty members present and participating, the Synod adopted the recommendations of its Advisory Committee with the exception of the last. The fifth professor was not dismissed, but was sent a "letter of admonition and clarification of his status."[3]

After this "deep and painful" surgery at the seminary only one person with regular faculty member status remained. He was Dr. M.J. Wyngaarden, Professor of Old Testament at the school since 1924.[4] Also remaining was Professor Extraordinary H. Schultze, who was teaching in the New Testament department. So the faculty was almost totally wiped out. Contributing to this state of affairs were other actions the synod was called upon to take. Dr. C. Bouma was given honorable emeritation because of continuing ill health. Dr. S. Volbeda, also in ill health, was granted honorable emeritation as well.

Rebuilding the Faculty

Appointments were made at once to the depleted faculty. Interim appointments were given to Dr. John H. Kromminga in Church History, to Professor R.B. Kuiper in Practical Theology, and to Dr. Henry Stob in Apologetics and Ethics. Dr. G.C. Berkouwer of The Netherlands and Dr. N.B. Stonehouse of Westminster were also appointed, but they did not see their way clear to accept. The Synod instructed the Board of Trustees of Calvin College and Seminary to appoint a president of the seminary for the ensuing year. R.B. Kuiper was appointed Acting President. Thus he became head of a third recognized Reformed institution, under circumstances which could hardly be called desirable. He served as Acting President and then President until his retirement in 1956.

R.B.'s firm and experienced administrative hand served Calvin Seminary well in these four years. Of very special importance was the continuing work of rebuilding the faculty. After his many years of service as a seminary professor and faculty chairman he had positive ideas regarding the qualifications of teachers in a theological seminary of Reformed persuasion. He imparted his ideas to the Board of Trustees and he laid them out in public in *The Banner* of May 15, 1953, prior to the meeting of synod in June, when further appointments would be made.

The seminary professor, wrote R.B., should be "truly godly" and "truly learned." By the latter requirement he meant a "broad liberal arts education as well as thorough theological training." Then we come to what R.B. Kuiper felt was of supreme urgency in the choice of seminary professors. He spelled it out as he stressed the point that the teachers of future ministers "must be thoroughly sound in doctrine. But that is not enough. No man should be permitted to teach at Calvin Seminary who does not possess a consuming zeal for the Reformed faith . . . He must be truly militant in his defense of the Reformed faith against heresy." To serve thus the professor "must be characterized by contemporaneity; that is, he must have a thorough acquaintance with present-day theological thought, both Reformed and otherwise."

This was for R.B. the true test to be applied to men considered for appointment to the seminary faculty, leaders in the church. If any person did not reveal positive signs of meeting this standard, he should not be permitted to teach at Calvin Seminary, as R.B. himself stated. If one is to understand the role that R.B. Kuiper played in the rebuilding of Calvin Seminary in those years, this point must never be forgotten. It is the key to all his evaluations and judgments of men involved in the work of the seminary. To what extent R.B.'s thinking prevailed in every appointment to the faculty is uncertain. He was an influential voice in the making of these appointments, but he surely was not the only voice. Other faculty members, members of the Board of Trustees, and the delegates to various synods were all involved. R.B.'s insistence on a robust and aggressive commitment to the Reformed faith did not mesh well with certain notions of academic freedom that were espoused by some in the church.

The word "militant" often appeared in R.B.'s speech and writing. He was in dead earnest about this. He would not settle for a less explicit adjective, like the word *diligent*. There were those who preferred the word *diligent* in describing the work of the professors in their exposition and defense of the faith. They said the word militant sounded too belligerent. R.B. would not accept the finer sounding word. He was thoroughly committed to the Pauline principle that the leaders in the church must fight the good fight of faith. His thinking on this score came out clearly when he wrote, "In the distinctiveness of Calvin College and Seminary lies their reason for existence. It follows that they have no more important task than that of maintaining their distinctiveness . . . If Calvin College and Seminary are to maintain their identity and to justify their continued existence, they will have to contend earnestly for the faith once for all delivered to the saints. More militancy to them!"[5] This emphasis, so typical of R.B. Kuiper, appeared under the heading "Our Distinctiveness" in his report to the Board of Trustees in May 1953, when he wrote, "In my February report I listed several requisites for teaching at Calvin Seminary. Prominent among them was militancy in the defense of the Reformed faith against modern error in all its numerous forms. I fervently hope and pray that Synod in choosing members of the seminary faculty will give serious consideration to that requisite."

Could men be found who met the standards that R.B. articulated so plainly? He had worked side by side at Westminster with men who met such qualifications to a high degree, and he would love to stock the rebuilding faculty at his alma mater with such people. In the brief time that R.B. was head of Calvin Seminary he worked hard to get the kind of men he felt the theological school needed. At the same time he battled to keep off the teaching staff men who did not meet his standards. He often said that one of the achievements of his four years at Calvin Seminary was to keep certain people off the faculty, people who sometimes had strong supporters within and outside the school.

Appointments to the faculty were made, in addition to those made in 1952. New appointees were as follows: Rev. Martin Monsma (Practical Theology), Rev. Carl G. Kromminga (Practical Theology), Dr. Ralph Stob (New Testament), Dr. Herman Kuiper (R.B.'s brother, Dogmatics), Rev. Marten H. Woudstra (Old Testament), Rev. Harold Dekker (Missions), and Dr. Fred H. Klooster (Dogmatics). Professor Extraordinary H. Schultze took on more teaching responsibilities in the New Testament department.

Progressive Steps

During R.B.'s tenure Calvin Seminary not only moved forward in rebuilding its faculty, it also took steps forward in other ways. An innovation that proved popular with the students was the introduction of a course in church music taught by a member of the college faculty. On another front course work was introduced in a field where R.B. recognized special need. He felt strongly that seminary students should be instructed in a deepened understanding of the mental and emotional states of people, and therefore a course in Pastoral Psychology or Psychiatry or Counselling was highly desirable. The school took advantage of a visit to America by Dr. J. Waterink of the Free University of Amsterdam and engaged him to teach a course in this field in 1954. Progress was also made in correcting an inadequacy in the seminary library, a deficiency brought to the school's attention by the American Association of Theological Schools. Surely not the least important forward step taken in those years was the decision by the Synod of 1955 to erect a new seminary building as a fitting memorial to mark the centennial of the Christian Reformed Church in the year 1957.

A Significant Address

A highlight of R.B.'s presidency of Calvin Seminary was an address he delivered at the convocation of the school in September of 1955. The address, entitled "A Confessional Seminary," furnishes us with the product of R.B. Kuiper's mature reflection on an important subject. This timely speech sought to answer the question how "we of the Seminary are to evaluate the confessions," that is, the three Forms of Unity of the Reformed churches more specifically. The confessions, he declared, must not be *overvalued*, nor must they be *undervalued*. We overvalue them when we neglect to honor the difference in the authority of the Scriptures as compared to that of the confessions. The Bible is infallible and timeless, terms which cannot be applied to the confessions, highly as we must prize them. R.B. referred as example to Article 36 of the Confession of Faith (Belgic Confession), which article the church had to revise because the original rendering taught Erastianism, the government of the church by the state. An illustration of under-valuing the confessions is found in the way in which many Modernists regard the confessions as relics of a past age, relics that no longer speak meaningfully to today's church.

This carefully phrased address concludes with twelve "pointed paragraphs" that laid out what R.B. saw as implications for the instruction given at Calvin Seminary. We present several of them here, in abbreviated form but in R.B.'s own words.

Portrait of Professor R.B. Kuiper hanging in Westminster Seminary.

We teach the Word of God rather than the confessions. This by no means rules out the confessions from our teaching, but we teach them simply because we deem them to be Scriptural.

We must in our interpretation of Scripture give due weight to the illumination of the historic church by the Spirit of truth, of which illumination the confessions are a prime product.

In our instruction we may not contradict the confessions. It hardly needs to be said that I am not referring to such minor questions as to who wrote the Epistle to the Hebrews . . . .

Perhaps all the great confessions of the Christian church, also those of the Reformed churches, were written in opposition to error . . . . It follows that one of the most solemn duties for a confessional seminary is to combat theological error; in other words, to engage in the militant defense of the faith.

While we may not in our teaching go contrary to the confessions, we may well go beyond them. It is even our duty to bring forth new things out of the treasure of the Word of God.

Being bound by the confessions does not restrict the freedom of those who teach at Calvin Seminary. Many of today's advocates of "academic freedom" are really insisting on academic license. May we never forget that true freedom is always freedom under law.

To Europe Again

In 1950 R.B. had gone to Europe to represent the Orthodox Presbyterian Church at the Second Plenary Congress of the International Council of Christian Churches meeting in Geneva. Five years later he went to Europe again, this time representing Calvin Seminary at the seventy-fifth anniversary celebration of the Free Reformed University of Amsterdam. It was a grand event covering three days, October 19, 20 and 21, 1955, and drew huge crowds, with well-wishers, official and otherwise, coming from near and far. Dignitaries from government and the academic world abounded, as well as plain folk who out of conviction had supported the Christian university faithfully.

The impressive affair was featured in the Christian national weekly newsmagazine De Spiegel with a well-illustrated lead article "Uit Geloof En Gehoorzaamheid" (Out of Faith and

Obedience). In the seventy-five years of its existence the university had grown from its beginnings with a faculty of five and a student body of five to a faculty of more than one hundred and students numbering more than two thousand. At the time of the celebration a new site had been procured and new buildings were being erected.

R.B. conveyed greetings from Calvin Seminary and the Board of Trustees to a large audience. He also read a special message from Calvin College. He had opportunity to speak about Calvin College and Seminary in a radio address. In his speech of greeting he congratulated the university on its coming into existence as a Calvinistic seat of learning, on its continued existence for seventy-five years despite all sorts of opposition and obstacles, and on the manner in which it had flourished and was continuing to prosper. Then he said he had two wishes for the school. First of all, he said, may the school "abide on the foundation that was laid in 1880. You founded the Free University 'op Gereformeerden grondslag!' May it never depart from that foundation . . . My second wish is that on that foundation the Free University may continue to build and build and build. May it be truly progressive as well as soundly conservative. As I said previously, the tower that you began to build in 1880 will never be completed. The task you undertook seventy-five years ago will never be finished. A Reformed university, like a Reformed church, must keep on reforming—and advancing. May you, therefore, ever bring forth new things as well as old out of the treasure of divine revelation, both special and general. And may you continue to do that unto distant generations, yea until Christ returns to perfect His kingdom."

Amsterdam had received him most cordially, R.B. reported. He carried these pleasant memories to the end of his life. He was spared from learning that the Free University did indeed depart from the "Gereformeerden grondslag" (Reformed foundation) when just a few years after R.B.'s death the school took the word Reformed out of its statement of basis. In its extensive commentary on the seventy-fifth anniversary celebration *De Spiegel* had commented on the dangers that lurked in the school's prosperity and prestige. The magazine had been prophetic.

Choosing R.B.'s Successor

It would be highly satisfying to declare that R.B.'s four years at Calvin Seminary ended in a way that could have allowed him to feel that the school was in good health, and that he had achieved pretty much what he knew was necessary to assure the genuinely Reformed training of ministers for years to come. The writer would personally like to leave that impression. But the simple fact is that such an impression would not be correct.

Not that R.B. was without strong supporters. Such support was well stated in a letter R.B. received from a pastor who had read the president's report to the Board of Trustees in May of 1953. This pastor, a member of the Board, wrote as follows:

> I was especially interested in your comments about the distinctiveness of our teaching in the seminary. I agree with you 100%. If we don't dare to dot the i's and cross the t's we are sunk as a denomination. To be specifically Reformed is the duty of both the minister in the pulpit and the professor in the seminary. As a minister of the gospel I know what it means to buck dispensationalism and modernism and especially arminianism with which many of our people seem to be afflicted. I believe the seminary must take the bull of all deviations from the truth by the horns and make Reformed truth live in the minds and hearts of our future ministers.

Many students attending Calvin Seminary in those four years expressed warm appreciation for the instruction they received from R.B. Kuiper. One graduate wrote thus:

> I am convinced that, though all the professors at Calvin Seminary have played a significant part in my education, and have consequently called forth my respect for them—nevertheless, I wish to say that no single person has meant more to my training in the hands of God than you, Rev. Kuiper. And thus it is with gratitude to God, rather than eulogy to man, that I hereby convey but a word of appreciation to you for the inspiration which you have been in my life. The classes which I had under you, though they were regrettably few, are unforgettable. Your pedagogical methods were such to make the most lethargic student sense the vitality of Reformed theology.

R.B. was honored at the request that he deliver the address at the commencement exercises of Calvin College and Seminary at the time he retired from the presidency of the seminary. He delivered an address that bore the clear R.B. Kuiper stamp. Under the title "Was Pilate Right?" he dealt with the question that Pontius Pilate threw at Jesus, "What is truth?"—a text he had often preached on. "Pilate meant to say," said R.B., "that truth is unimportant, that truth is *unknowable*." He spoke earnestly of the saving truth that is revealed to us in the Scriptures, the truth we know as the Reformed faith. But he felt constrained to voice his "fear that even we of the Christian Reformed Church are rapidly losing our sense of the importance of truth." Of special interest was the like concern he expressed in his last report to the Board of Trustees as he spoke of "a measure of disappointment with the present interest of the seminary community in distinctive Calvinism."

The clearest signal pointing to frustration that R.B. experienced as he finished his tenure at Calvin Seminary was his failure to see a man in whom he had full confidence chosen to succeed him as president. The selection process turned out to be a struggle. R.B. had a hand in the choice of his successor. He was one member of a Nominating Committee composed of members of the Board and of the faculty. The committee presented a trio of names to the Board of Trustees at its meeting held in February of 1956. The Board rejected the nomination. The Nominating Committee submitted another trio of names to the May meeting of the Board. It was almost another rejection. The Board added three names to the nomination and out of the six candidates two names were chosen for submission to the forthcoming synod.

The struggle continued at synod. First of all it was decided that the body should not elect a president from the nomination made by the Board because it had not been submitted in time, according to the rules covering such appointments. But then the synod rejected a proposal by its Advisory Committee that the Executive Committee of the Board of Trustees appoint a member of the faculty as Acting President for a year. So the tussle continued. The Advisory Committee then came with a proposal that the synod elect an Acting President to serve for a year from a nomination of Prof. J.H. Kromminga, Rev. N.J.

Monsma and Prof. Henry Stob. Synod rejected the part about the Acting President. But what about the rules referred to above? Synod decided to suspend the rules. A new nomination was proposed and approved, namely, "the present eligible members of the faculty who hold the rank of professor or associate professor." Dr. J.H. Kromminga was elected. Thus after a tortuous process the church chose a man who would hold this important post for a quarter of a century.

Chapter 17

The Man and His Wit

He was a man of humor and of wit, yes, of both. Sometimes that which passes for humor is fairly witless, with laughter won by dwelling on that which is bawdy or inane. Not so with R.B. His humor could send a highly educated and cultured gentleman like J. Gresham Machen into high glee, and a delicate touch of the amusing could bring a smile to the face of the average listener in the pew. Often his humor was so sly that even his wife of many years could not tell whether she should take him seriously. The combination of a brilliant mind, lively personality and an aspersion of all that he sometimes called "high-falutin" or "put on" gave him a capacity for humor that few could surpass.

Boiling the Puppy

One of those surprising twists came not long after our first child was born. She was R.B.'s first grandchild. At the time there was much insistence on the need to sterilize most everything a baby might touch. Grandpa Kuiper was highly amused at this whole business. He thought it was much overdone. One day we were talking in R.B.'s presence about things we might do for the child's entertainment. We agreed that it would be great to get a puppy for her. R.B. chimed in by saying, "You can't have a puppy for that child."

"Why not?" we asked in some surprise.

He answered, "Because you'd have to boil it ten minutes first."

R.B. entered into a state of euphoria at the birth of his first grandchild. We often said that she somehow filled the place that had been left so painfully vacant by the death of Kathryn Junia many years before. No grandchild could be the object of more loving attention than our first baby received from R.B. When she became a toddler and the family visited a restaurant, he loved to take her hand for a stroll so that the patrons could admire the little girl with the auburn hair and the blue eyes. When she was just a few months old I had occasion to comment at a Westminster alumni gathering on R.B.'s feelings about his granddaughter. In my few remarks I said that there was reason for concern about the doctrinal soundness of the seminary, because since the first grandchild had come into the life of the Professor of Practical Theology he had begun to waver precariously on the doctrine of original sin. He took the sally in good grace.

R.B. corresponded faithfully with his daughter when she was doing postgraduate study at the University of Michigan. His letters to her, written from Philadelphia, often contained highly amusing tidbits. In a letter he wrote shortly before she was to come home for the Christmas holidays he said, "As the monkey said when the lawnmower cut off his tail, 'It won't be long now . . .'"

In another letter he told the story of an Arabian sheik who on his deathbed gave instructions for the disposition of his estate of seventeen camels. The oldest of his three sons was to receive one-half of the estate, the second son one-third and the youngest son one-ninth. The division of the estate of seventeen camels in the manner prescribed by the deceased posed a real problem. The three sons simply didn't know what to do. Finally they decided to call in a noted sage to help them. The wise man came on his camel, listened to the story of the three sons, and then went to work. He added his camel to the seventeen, making for a total of eighteen animals. Then the oldest son was awarded his one-half, nine camels. The second son received his one-third, six camels. The third son got his one-ninth, two camels. That totalled seventeen camels. His job done, the sage took his stipend and rode off on his camel. It need hardly be said that daughter Marietta greatly enjoyed getting letters from her father.

The period of time in which I courted his daughter was

educational for me as I slowly began to understand something of R.B.'s extraordinary sense of humor. I learned a bit one evening when R.B. was getting ready to retire after he had been in the kitchen helping his wife prepare a chicken for the next day's Sunday dinner. As he concluded his chores and started ascending the stairs for the night he said to us, "I hope the house doesn't burn down tonight." We had no idea as to why that had suddenly popped into his head, but we soon learned as he added, "Because if it does we won't have any chicken tomorrow."

The meat at another dinner at the Kuipers was not chicken, as the young guests learned. R.B. and Mrs. Kuiper were entertaining the children of some friends of theirs. As R.B. was cutting the meat he casually asked the children, "Did you ever eat horsemeat?" The youngsters were mildly surprised at the question but passed it off by saying that they didn't think they had ever eaten it. When the children returned to their home, their mother asked them what they had had to eat at the Kuipers. To her astonishment the children replied matter-of-factly, "Horsemeat." The parents didn't know just what to make of the children's report, but they had come to know R.B. and suspected it was some of his funny stuff.

Our home in northern New Jersey for ten years received many a visit from Pa and Ma Kuiper. Not far from us was the town of Suffern, located just across the line in lower New York State. The name of the town caught R.B.'s attention and a story came forth. The tale he told had to do with a couple traveling by car in northern New Jersey. They lost their way and as they were driving along slowly, trying to get back on the right track, they spotted a boy sitting on a rail fence. They stopped, and as the driver pointed his finger in a forward direction he called out to the boy, "Suffern?" The boy replied, "Naw. I'm jus' sittin' here."

"Crazy Jokes" Not His Cup of Tea

One never knew when and how R.B.'s sense of humor might come to expression. One way in which his sense of humor did not function very well was in what have been called "crazy jokes." The game of "knock, knock" is an illustration. R.B.

just could not get the hang of this type of humor. Maybe that is to his credit. This silly game was at the peak of its popularity when the family took a trip from Philadelphia to Michigan by way of Canada. I was a guest on the trip; we were not yet married. The itinerary included a visit at the place where the famous Dionne quintuplets lived in northern Ontario. During the course of the journey R.B. heard a number of "knock, knock" jokes told by the younger passengers in the car. One of these bits of humor came about when Dr. Dafoe, the quints' physician, appeared in his car at the entrance to the compound around the special residence of the five little girls. "Knock, knock," came the opening words.

"Who's there?" was the proper response in this "crazy" humor.

"Dafoe."

"Dafoe who?"

"Dafoe is in the gate," came the finishing quip.

R.B. tried his hand at concocting "knock, knock" jokes. He was ordinarily a past master at fabricating jokes. But his efforts with the "crazy jokes" just did not come off. His mind simply did not work that way. He heard another good example of this type of humor, but the key still eluded him. This other piece of jollity that was so baffling to R.B. opened with the usual "Knock, knock" and "Who's there?" The word "Archibald" followed.

"Archibald who?"

"Archibald yet?" So ended the joke as did R.B's miscarriages of humor so far as the "crazy jokes" were concerned. These jokes were too quirky for him.

Some Humor Off Limits

The ability to laugh is "a precious gift of God to man." So R.B. wrote in an article entitled "A Prevalent Sin."[1] He said further that in the stress and strain of life it is dangerous not to use this gift. But then he added that the gift can easily be abused so that it becomes something silly or even irreverent. This was the "prevalent sin" the *Banner* article was all about.

Humor involving the name of God or the Bible or anything

else that Christians regard as sacred was definitely off limits for R.B. His humor never strayed into these areas that were out of bounds for him. He reacted unfavorably when a colleague of his told a joke about the arrival of a former U.S. president at the pearly gates of heaven. In the joke as told the president was asked by an angel what he could contribute if he were allowed to enter into heaven. He replied that he could write constitutions. He was told to submit a sample. He did. After a short while the angel returned with the sample constitution and declared that it was not satisfactory, because God did not want to be vice-president. The joke elicited loud laughter, especially from those who did not admire the former president. But R.B. did not laugh, even though he was not an admirer of the former chief of state. This definitely was not his brand of humor.

Nor was death a subject for humor for this man of wit. That is fully understandable when we remember the pain he suffered in the death of his little daughter. And humor that used the Bible flippantly or irreverently was strictly ruled out. In the article referred to above R.B. spoke of those who quote Scripture "irrelevantly and quite unexpectedly in the midst of otherwise inane remarks. When this is done by those who believe that the Bible is the verbally inspired Word of God, my blood boils." Of course, humor that did not deal irreverently with the Bible and had a good thrust was another matter. R.B. liked to tell a story that illustrated gross ignorance of the contents of the Bible. At a meeting of Sunday School teachers, according to the story, one of the group referred to Dan and Beersheba as places in Palestinian geography. Another teacher spoke up saying, "Dan and Beersheba aren't names of places. They are the names of a husband and his wife, just like Sodom and Gomorrah."

R.B. never engaged in so-called barnyard or barroom humor. In all the years that I heard countless jokes and funny things from his lips, I never once heard him tell a "dirty story." He was deeply annoyed when ministers of the gospel told such stories. He was also annoyed at the liberties taken by some masters of ceremonies at wedding affairs. Not infrequently these people would use the occasion to tell a number of off-color jokes. At such times R.B. did not join in the merriment.

Marriage, of course, has to be the subject of much humor that can be highly amusing. Always alert to the comic face of life, R.B. told many a joke about marriage. However, his humor never put marriage in a bad light nor cheapened it. After all, he could hardly speak with even a hint of derision about a bond that the Bible likens to the blessed relationship between Christ and His church.

So his humor involving marriage was always gently bantering. He liked to tell a story about a couple who had been married twenty-five years in a bond known by many to have been a happy one. The husband was asked to reveal the secret of their successful marriage. "Oh, that's simple," he said. "When we were married we made an agreement that I as the man would make all the major decisions and my wife would make all the minor decisions. It so happens that to date we have not had a major decision to make."

R.B. told about a wedding ceremony he once conducted. When the ceremony was concluded the groom asked him, "Now what do I owe you?"

"You don't *owe* me anything," R.B. answered, stressing the word *owe*.

"Thank you very much," said the groom, and he went off happily with his bride.

After another wedding the groom asked, "What is your fee?"

R.B. replied with a question of his own, "What is it worth to you?"

The groom dug into his pocket and gave the preacher three quarters. Then that groom went off happily with his inexpensive bride. R.B. never again responded in that way to a groom's question about the fee.

An added reason for R.B.'s respect for marriage was his high regard and love for his wife. He always spoke of her with words of unstinting praise. One facet of her character afforded him some amusement. She liked animals as long as they were at a respectable distance from her, as in a storybook. This was so even though she had been reared on a farm. Some kinds of animals she didn't like at all. This fact gave the family a merry time one day at a picnic at a roadside park in the lovely Pennsylvania countryside. At one point I happened to see R.B. struggling to suppress his laughter. I edged close to him and asked what was so funny. He told me to look up. I did and discovered that the tree under which we were picnicking was infested with caterpillars. For Mrs. Kuiper caterpillars were unseemly creatures that she could not tolerate, in a class with snakes and lizards and toads. Fortunately R.B. was able to hide his amusement from his wife and the picnic went very well, with Mrs. Kuiper blissfully unaware of the threat that hung over her head.

Naturally it would be wrong to assume that R.B. was always funny. In the scale of his life his ready sense of humor made for a fine balance with the high and intense seriousness with which he studied, preached and taught the riches of God's Word. Then again there were many occasions when humor was simply not in order. This was the case when I entered the Kuiper home one day to find R.B. seated in a favorite easy chair nursing a miserable cold. His head was stuffed up, his nose dripping and his eyes watering. Sympathetically I asked him how he felt. His answer was one eloquent word—"Rotten." I know that I have never heard that word spoken with greater conviction

When His Wit Was Sharp

His ability to tell a good and appropriate story matched his widely recognized ability to make a good and appropriate speech. It was not only Dr. Machen who greatly enjoyed R.B.'s humor. Professor Murray was another who sometimes almost fell off his chair in laughter at his colleague's stories. The seminary group enjoyed a story about a Roman Catholic priest and a Jewish rabbi as they sat at dinner together. The priest was enjoying a delicious piece of ham. The priest couldn't resist twitting his Jewish table partner, who was bound by the dietary restrictions of his religion. "Friend," said the priest, "when are you going to enjoy a delicious piece of ham like this?" "At your wedding," was the rabbi's return thrust.

So R.B. regaled the seminary community with his wit. On another occasion he told a story to illustrate the meticulous scholarship of the professors. Attention to details characterized their work, R.B. said. He made his point by telling about a fishing trip taken by two of his colleagues. The two professors rowed their boat to several locations but they caught no fish.

Finally they anchored at a place where fishing was good. When they had caught all they wanted they pulled up the anchor and started rowing to shore. Suddenly professor number one said regretfully, "We should have marked the spot where we caught all the fish."

"I took care of that," said professor number two.

"How did you do that?" asked professor number one in some surprise.

"It was simple," said professor number two; "I had a piece of chalk with me and so I put a mark on the side of the boat at the very spot where we caught the fish."

His unfailing wit served well at an annual alumni dinner held at commencement time. All those present were very much aware of the resignation from the faculty of a professor whose reasons for leaving were hardly adequate, in R.B.'s view of the matter. As chairman of the faculty R.B. was asked to make a few remarks. His comments dwelt in the main on R.B.'s early association with Westminster Seminary. He told about the excitement of being on the first faculty of the school and about his leaving after one year. He dwelt on the point that his departure at that time was one of the best things that ever happened to Westminster. This was so because the vacancy brought about by his departure was filled by John Murray, who proved to be such a superb teacher of Systematic Theology. "So," he said pointedly, "my departure was a very good thing for the seminary." The professor leaving the school at the time was also present at the alumni dinner. What was he thinking as the chairman of the faculty spoke?

The Fluent Speaker

His wit was never sharper than it was when he responded to an introduction he was given as he was about to speak to a church group in the Philadelphia area. The one introducing him was a senior seminarian, a bright chap, but one has to wonder about his sense of propriety as he introduced his professor. He said that he had heard more than once that Professor Kuiper was a fluent speaker. That word *fluent* caught his attention and he decided to get its exact meaning. Having studied the Hebrew language in seminary, he felt he had to find the root word in the adjective *fluent*. On searching the dictionary he discovered the root of the word. It was the word *flue*, which the dictionary described as "a passage for hot air."

Those in the audience wondered just how R.B. would handle that sally. They need not have wondered. As he rose to speak the first response was his usual one. He expressed his thanks for the introduction. Then he said he was reminded of a conversation he had recently with a man who had heard a sermon delivered by the student who had introduced R.B. The man had said to R.B., "He reminded me of you, but he was more fluent than you are." After Kuiper had finished his speech the student's comment was, "R.B. Kuiper is a hard man to get ahead of."

This student was not the only one to learn that fact about R.B. Kuiper. His responses to toastmasters or masters of ceremonies were unforgettable on occasion. Once he was introduced by a man who was exceptionally long-winded. R.B. was always straining at the leash when he had to speak. His patience was sorely tried as this man went on and on and on. Finally when R.B. got up to speak he thanked the toastmaster for his introduction and then said he was reminded of a story about a farmer feeding his hogs. The farmer had a visitor at hog-feeding time, a city-bred visitor. The farmer fed his hogs corn on the cob. As the visitor watched the pigs working on the ears of corn he said to the farmer, "Wouldn't it take them less time if you fed them shelled corn?" The farmer replied, "What's time to a hog?" Perhaps that master of ceremonies learned his lesson.

His response was more kindly but just as sharp at a convention banquet of the National Union of Christian Schools (later named Christian Schools International). He was introduced by a man who had been a student at Calvin College when R.B. was president of the school. He was also a superb humorist and in time was much in demand as a master of ceremonies. After he had appropriately introduced his former mentor at the Christian School convention banquet R.B. responded by saying this, "If the prophet Isaiah had told me when I was at Calvin College that this student would one day introduce me at a banquet of the National Union of Christian Schools, I would have said to the great prophet, 'You're a liar.'"

Some may think that this response violated R.B.'s own rule of not using biblical material in humor that might be regarded as irreverent. The point might be debatable. Those who feel thus might bear in mind that if one enjoys a broad and solid reputation he can afford a bit of inconsistency.

A Story About Hypocrisy

No preacher can ignore the subject of hypocrisy in his sermonizing. R.B. did not neglect the subject. In his ample store of sermon illustrations was a story that scored high in its exposure of hypocrisy. The story was about a world famous circus magnate. This man of circus fame grew up in a home that was situated above the family grocery store. As a boy he had certain chores to do before the store opened for business each day. The usual morning routine went somewhat as follows. After the lad had been downstairs for a short while attending to his chores the father called down to him and asked, "Son, have you put chalk in the sugar?"

"Yes, I did, Father," the lad replied.

Then the father called again, "Have you put water in the vinegar?"

"Yes, Father," came the answer.

"And have you put dust in the pepper?"

"Yes, Father; I've taken care of everything."

"Good, son. Now you can come up for morning prayers." With illustrations like that it is no wonder that people loved to hear R.B. Kuiper preach.

Whether it was the average man in the pew or the learned theologian, all were captivated by R.B.'s humor. Once the very able Anglican cleric Philip E. Hughes was speaking to a group of ministers and theological professors in Grand Rapids, Michigan. As he began his speech he said he had to tell the story by which R.B. Kuiper had introduced him at an earlier speaking event in Grand Rapids, a story at which he had been highly amused since he as a Calvinist was somewhat of a rarity among Anglican clergymen. In this story R.B. had told about two men who were taking a stroll through a cemetery. As these men looked at the inscriptions on the tombstones, one of them suddenly cried out,

"Here's something different, really different."

"What is it?" his friend asked.

"Here are two men in one grave," came the reply.

"Two men in one grave? That's strange."

"Well, this is what it says on this tombstone: Here lies an Anglican and a Calvinist."

The capacity for delicate self-depreciating humor is commonly looked upon as a mark of a real person of wit. R.B. had this capacity. An example of such humor is found in a letter in which he had something to say about the behavior of a great-granddaughter. He wrote, "Janie is developing wonderfully. She likes to play with Mom but does not yet have full confidence in me, which may well be evidence of high intelligence." This delightful pleasantry turned out to be prophetic. The child became a top student throughout her school career, from kindergarten through college. It is not hard to see where she got some of that "high intelligence." Some of it came from her great-grandfather, a man of rare wit.

Chapter 18

Productive Retirement

"We keep the garbage can in the garage." This was R.B.'s stock answer when anyone asked him whether they owned a television set. The Kuipers didn't want a TV set and they didn't need one. They didn't want it because they felt that much of what appeared on TV would be a waste of their time, and not a small amount of such material would be offensive to their moral sensitivities. They didn't need it because they had plenty to do.

For relaxation R.B. and Mrs. Kuiper enjoyed the stereophonic radio-phonograph they purchased, recommended to them by a friend in the business as the best available. And they enjoyed playing games with the children and grandchildren as well as with close friends. R.B. often had a great time at a game of Rook, and he was good at it. He played to win, but could lose with grace. Of course, he never ceased to be the avid and interesting conversationalist in discussions of matters relating to church or state.

Another source of relaxation was his flowers. He maintained a modest but attractive bed of them in the backyard. Dressed in quite unprofessional clothes and wearing his sloppy gardening hat, he was often seen tending carefully to his colorful patch of flowers. At one point in his career as a gardener he was spoken to as follows, "I never met a preacher who looked less like one than you do." He took the remark as a high compliment.

But the main story of this period of his life, as in every previous period, does not have to do with fun and games, nor with pleasant conversations and flowers, much as R.B. relished such things. Again the main story has to do with labors in and

183

for Christ's kingdom. R.B. was still very much in demand as a preacher, and as speaker under a great variety of circumstances and auspices. It was most interesting, for instance, to read a letter from Lear, Inc., Grand Rapids industrial firm, in which favorable comment is made on a talk R.B. gave to the Bible Fellowship at the plant. The letter, dated May 1, 1958, reads in part as follows, "The simplicity and clarity with which you presented the rather controversial subject of 'God's Sovereignty and Man's Responsibility' was not only appreciated, but very edifying."

The Presses Roll

R.B.'s productivity in the final decade of his life was demonstrated especially in the books that came from his pen—five of them with the last one published posthumously. This was the prime goal he had in view when he retired from Westminster in 1952. He was itching to get those books out, books that would, he hoped, promote the faith that was so precious to him. His books were not aimed at the academic community first of all, although members of this elite group can read these works with profit. R.B. wanted to get books of a pronounced Reformed stamp into the hands of the plain people of the church. So he wrote with them especially in view. And he succeeded to a high degree. Adjectives like "clear," "lucid" and even "pellucid" abound in reviews of his books and in appreciative letters he received.

The Glorious Body of Christ was the first of the five books to appear. Comprising what first appeared as a long series of articles in *The Presbyterian Guardian*, the volume contains fifty-three chapters, each one usually five pages or so in length. This makes the book highly readable to the person who finds it difficult to read long discourses on thought-provoking themes. The book covers just about every facet of the character, work and worship of the church, not of any particular denomination, but the "catholic" church of the Apostles' Creed. This broad appeal of the book is accented by its translation into Spanish and projected translation into Chinese. Called R.B.'s "masterpiece" by Professor John Murray, the entire book is eminently worth reading. At a time when worship services are often trivialized by self-serving gimmickry and innovations, the chapters on the "Essence" and the "Quality" of Corporate Worship are highly salutary reading, especially for pastors and elders.

Then came *For Whom Did Christ Die?* This book sets forth plainly and unashamedly the Calvinist teaching of Limited Atonement, or, as R.B. preferred to call it, Particular Atonement or Definite Atonement. Particularism, over against unrestricted universalism and inconsistent universalism, is the view of the *Divine Design of the Atonement* that is embraced by "those churches and persons that adhere uncompromisingly to historic Calvinism" (Introduction), and this is the view R.B. presents in his usual forceful style. But he is not just repeating the simplistic statement that says that "Christ died only for the elect." The statement is not adequate, says R.B. To be sure, "God's design in the atonement was indeed in a most real sense particular," but it clearly was "in no less real sense universal." What R.B. means by that statement, probably surprising to some Calvinists, is made clear in the chapters on "Scriptural Particularism" and "Scriptural Universalism."

A Renewed Plea

In the same year R.B. produced *To Be or Not To Be Reformed.* Subtitle of the book is "Whither the Christian Reformed Church?" The book is not a jeremiad on the future of the Christian Reformed Church. He wrote, "But I also see within the church much good which, I hope, may be augmented" (Preface). Notice the *but* at the beginning of that sentence. This follows these words, "Am I of the opinion that the Christian Reformed Church is beset by specific perils at this time? Of that I am certain. I see such perils within the church and without, and to them I would call attention." He concluded the paragraph by saying, "And so this volume, while in no way a prediction, is meant to provide both warning and encouragement." Realizing full well that the church could no longer find its strength in its ethnic isolation, R.B. pressed for a fuller awareness of the church's real strength in its distinctiveness. And that distinctiveness lies in the church's Reformed character, its place "in the great and glorious tradition of Warfield and Hodge, Bavinck and Kuiper, the Westminster Assembly and the Synod of Dordt, Calvin, Augustine, and, to cap the climax, Paul."[1] So the book concludes with the plea, "Let us steadfastly refuse to detract even a little from our Reformed heritage. Shall we and our children not much rather enter more fully than ever before upon its enjoyment? What we need is not to become a little less Reformed, but much more so."[2]

We pause to ask a question. Would R.B. have expended all the labor involved in producing this book if he thought all was well with his mother church? The answer seems obvious. Why a second book about being Reformed? Thirty-three years before, we recall, he wrote *As To Being Reformed*. Then he underscored "the imminent peril in which we American Calvinists are of losing our precious Reformed heritage, and the supreme importance of our holding it fast." In the later book of similar title he writes after his experiences in the Orthodox Presbyterian Church and its struggle to maintain a Reformed witness, and after he has once again viewed the Christian Reformed Church at close range for seven years. Of these seven years the year 1957 had been the centennial anniversary of the Christian Reformed Church. So he felt deeply constrained to put forth this second plea to the church to maintain her distinctiveness. He felt he had just cause for issuing this renewed plea.

The book's observations regarding the Christian Reformed Church are never severe or unloving. R.B. wrote as one who loved the church that nurtured him. But he did say some things that ought to arrest the attention of every serious-minded member of the Christian Reformed Church. Let these members of Christ's body pay heed as R.B. declared, "Perhaps the most serious weakness of the Christian Reformed Church at present is a dearth of doctrinal discernment. Generally speaking our people cannot distinguish between truth and error as they should. Most of them know very little and are practically unaware of the prevalent heresies of the day."[3] Such comments are definitely in line with the experience of the writer of this book in the years that he was closely associated with R.B. after his return to Grand Rapids in 1952. R.B.'s conversations with respect to the Christian Reformed Church were often tinged with pessimism as to its future as a distinctively Reformed church.

At the same time his vision regarding the future of the Christian Reformed Church was not altogether gloomy. He also saw signs of hope. One of these was in the large number of Christian schools flourishing in communities of Christian Reformed believers. He saw another hopeful omen in the big influx of Calvinistic immigrants following the Second World War, immigrants who came from the Reformed churches of The Netherlands. This development, especially among the Christian Reformed Churches in Canada, fueled R.B.'s renewed hope because of the strong emphasis among these newcomers in the church on the mediatorial kingship of Christ as resolutely applied by them to the whole of life. This conviction and its faithful application were to R.B. an essential ingredient in the Reformed conception of faith and life.

Incidentally, the fact that the book concerned itself with one particular denomination in no way precluded an appeal to a much wider readership. One reviewer saw emphases in the book which "are of utmost value for the life of any branch of the visible church today."[4] A review written in Ireland stated that the book's contents were of concern to every true child of the Protestant Reformation. A reader in Australia wrote that the book had been a great help to him as he switched his membership from the Church of England to a Reformed church.

A Theology of Evangelism

When the book *God-Centered Evangelism* appeared in 1961 from the pen of R.B. Kuiper a very real need was met. The book deals with what may be called the main business of the church—evangelism. Its approach is unique. It has been used as a textbook in a number of schools. It has been translated into the Spanish language, as was also *The Glorious Body of Christ*. The significance of the title of the book is given explanation in the following quotation from the Preface.

> Sad to say, much of present-day evangelism is man-centered. Far too often the limelight is turned full upon the evangelist—his personality, his eloquence, his ability as an organizer, the story of his conversion, the hardships which he has endured, the number of his converts, in some instances the

miracles of healing allegedly performed by him. At other times attention is focused on those who are being evangelized—their large numbers, their sorry plight as exemplified by poverty, disease, and immorality, their supposed yearning for the gospel of salvation, and, worst of all, the good that is said to dwell in them and to enable them to exercise saving faith of their own free, although unregenerate, volition. And how often the welfare of man, whether temporal or eternal, is made the sole end of evangelism!

Hence the book seeks to place God in the forefront in the whole matter of evangelism. The book presents a "scriptural theology of evangelism," according to the subtitle. Significantly, therefore, all nineteen chapter headings begin with the word GOD. So there are chapters, for instance, on God the Author of Evangelism, God's Sovereign Election and Evangelism, God and the Scope of Evangelism, God and the Approach to Evangelism, God and Resistance to Evangelism. In the chapter on God and the Motive of Evangelism we find material that should whet the appetite of the reader. Getting down to "brass tacks," to use some of R.B.'s down-to-earth language, he issued a warning.

> We of today need to be on guard against selfish motivation in evangelism. The minister who would become a missionary to a backward people in order to escape the onerous task of preaching to an educated audience in the homeland is guilty of selfishness. So is the man or the woman who would bring the gospel to a distant land because of the halo which in the estimation of sentimental folk is wont to surround foreign missionaries. So is he or she who, troubled by an inferiority complex in civilized America, reckons that a sense of superiority over uncivilized Africans is a thing to be grasped. So is the missionary who places adventure above, or on a par with, evangelization. And the same is true of the person who engages in evangelism in order to make a display of personal piety.[5]

Elsewhere we read, "The Reformed faith provides the strongest and noblest motive for evangelism. Love for unworthy self and love for unlovely man are indeed worthy motives, but neither of these is the ultimate motive. The ultimate, hence the most compelling, motive must be love for the altogether adorable God."[6]

Pushing the Reformed Cause

The writing of books was not the only means R.B. used to promote the faith he so heartily loved and preached. He also wrote many articles. And many of these appeared in a new magazine that made its debut in 1951. It was called *Torch and Trumpet*, a name suggested by the story of Gideon and his band with their weapons of torches and trumpets. The name, reduced to "T 'n T" by many and to "Glow and Blow" by others, was later changed to *The Outlook*. This was not the only new magazine to make its appearance in Christian Reformed circles in that year. *The Reformed Journal* also entered the scene in 1951. In fact, the two papers came out almost simultaneously, just one month apart. This remarkable coincidence stirred much comment and speculation. Why these two new magazines at the same time? Did they represent "a deep difference of opinion suddenly breaking into the open?" In its opening article *Torch and Trumpet* declared that the sponsors of the magazine had no such conscious intent. The Reformed Fellowship, publishers of the magazine, made this declaration: "It seems very clear to us, the sponsors of *Torch and Trumpet*, that the method to be followed in seeking to further the interests of the Reformed faith will be quite different in the two journals. We are certain that this difference will become increasingly apparent as the issues appear."[7]

This difference became fully apparent to R.B. and he cast his lot with *Torch and Trumpet*. That he did this is in itself an item worthy of notice. R.B. was not a great joiner. He preferred to be his own spokesman, and he could not permit any association he might enter into to compromise his strong faith commitment in any way. Already in the second year of the magazine's existence he wrote a brief series of articles for the new publication. Then after his retirement many articles appeared over his signature. In his judgment the magazine was an effective instrument for the propagation of the Reformed faith. He served on the Editorial Committee for the last five and one-half years of his life.

The magazine was fortunate to have so able and seasoned a theologian as R.B. on board. He soon demonstrated his gifts and insights, as in the first article he wrote after retirement from Calvin Seminary. It was a review article on Dr. Harry R. Boer's book *That My House May Be Filled*, which was subtitled "A Study of Evangelism in the Christian Reformed Church." In his searching analysis of this study on evangelism by a missionary to Nigeria, R.B. makes a number of observations that say much about the writer of the book and about the writer of the review. He commended Boer for saying that the heart of the evangelist's message must be salvation by grace. But the book is marred, R.B. wrote, by a number of infelicitous and unacceptable assertions, even "several extreme statements." R.B.'s theological sensitivity rebelled at Boer's declaration, "We do not preach the gospel of the Reformed churches. We preach the gospel of the Lord Jesus Christ." And at this assertion, "The minister does not preach theology. He preaches *the gospel*." "How patently false an antithesis!" was R.B.'s terse judgment.[8]

"Withstand Beginnings" was the title of another piece of writing by R.B. The title is a translation of the Latin expression *Principiis Obsta!* What *beginnings* was R.B. talking about? He said that he had to admit almost blushingly that he was talking about the very unpopular thing called *heresy*. The article was the substance of an address delivered before a section of the Evangelical Theological Society, a scholarly group of which R.B. was a founder in 1949. The theme of the conference at which R.B. spoke was Scriptural Infallibility. The following arresting statement sums up the main thrust of the article: "He who sets up himself as judge as to what in the Bible is the authoritative Word of God and what is not, is not going to lose the Bible; he has already lost it. The very act of mere man's sitting in judgment on the Word of God constitutes rejection of the Word of God." As he concludes R.B. drives home his warning, "And so I plead with you: *Principiis obstemus*! Let us withstand beginnings! *Principiis diligenter obstemus*! Let us diligently withstand beginnings! *Principiis diligentissime obstemus*! Let us most diligently withstand beginnings!"[9]

"*Is the Glory Departing?*"

Nothing that R.B. Kuiper wrote for *Torch and Trumpet* drew more attention than the article he wrote in 1963 under the heading "Is the Glory Departing?" He made clear that he, referring to the word *Ichabod* uttered by the dying wife of Phineas (I Sam. 4:21), was not saying that the glory had departed from the Christian Reformed Church, nor was he asking whether it had departed. Rather, speaking of himself, he said, "Speaking the truth in love, he is in all seriousness raising the question whether the glory is not in danger, perhaps even in process, of departing from that church."[10]

This lengthy, carefully written article deserves attentive reading by anyone interested in the welfare of the church of Christ. The publishers of the magazine called the piece a "significant article" and made it available in pamphlet form. Reference is made here to a few developments in the church that R.B. dealt with.

Of importance was what R.B. had to say about the debate concerning the infallibility of Scripture that engaged the church and synod toward the end of the fifties and in the early sixties. A student at Calvin Seminary had written a piece entitled "Infallibility Questioned" in the student paper *Stromata*. The article created a stir in the church. The seminary president sought to clear the air by writing a paper on the subject "How Shall We Understand Infallibility?" He argued that the question before the church was "what was believed to be infallible, and how far that infallibility extended." Then he went on to say, "Granting that the Holy Spirit infallibly conveyed what He intended to teach, how shall we interpret Scriptural items which are on the periphery of that teaching?"[11]

Professor of Old Testament Dr. M.J. Wyngaarden was not at all satisfied with the president's paper and brought his objections to the Synod of 1959. R.B.'s sympathies were clearly with the professor, who was known to be a considerably better scholar than teacher. "Here let it be said," R.B. asserted in his article, "that the Christian Reformed Church owes a debt of gratitude to Dr. Martin J. Wyngaarden for bringing the issue to a head at the . . . Synod by way of protest and appeal. Nor is it

true, as many suppose, that Synod gave little heed to his conten-
tions. On the contrary, in effect it sustained several of them."[12]

On the Love of God

Another issue featured in R.B.'s article "Is the Glory
Departing?" had to do with a sharp debate that broke out in
reaction to an article written by the professor of Missions at
Calvin Seminary. The essay, appearing in *The Reformed
Journal* of December 1962, was entitled "God So Loved—All
Men," with cue taken from John 3:16. An extensive discussion
of the issues raised in the debate had come from R.B.'s pen at an
earlier date.[13] At no time did R.B. deny that God does indeed
love all men and not just the elect, as some theologians maintained. So R.B. dealt more carefully with the professor's position than some critics did. But he objected to identifying God's
love for the elect with His love for the non-elect. In a very real
sense God does love all men as He bestows upon all alike the
blessings of what is called common grace. But to claim that the
issue is settled by stating, as the professor had done, that "God's
love is love; it cannot be something else," is too simplistic an
answer to a difficult question. It does not do justice to the
teaching of Scripture regarding God's very special love for His
own.

Nor was Kuiper satisfied with the writer's insistence that
God's love for the elect and His love for the non-elect are the
same, the only difference being in *results*. Such teaching is at
odds with the reality of salvation by efficacious grace. R.B.
argued in much the same fashion in a second full article in the
debate.[14] He continued to press the point that God's love for His
own is a special love, even though we are faced with a mystery as
to how God distinguishes His love for His own from His love for
all men. The professor did distinguish between God's love for all
men as "redemptive" and His love for the elect as "redeeming,"
but the distinction is "confusing," R.B. found. It was no more
than a merely verbal answer to the problem, since the teacher of
Missions refused to allow for a qualitative distinction between
God's "redemptive" and His "redeeming" love. In a nutshell
these views taught that with the same love God loved some peo-

ple to heaven and others to hell. That was not the gospel of saving grace (or love) that R.B. had preached for so long and so fervently.

On God's Hate

Not surprisingly the debate on the love of God sparked debate on God's hate. An article appeared on the question "Does God *Hate* Some Men?" It was written by the professor of Apologetics and Ethics at Calvin Seminary. "As for me," wrote the professor, "I think that to ascribe hate of persons to God is to pervert the very thought of God. I believe that we are emphatically not permitted by the total witness of the Scriptures to say that God hates men in any distinct and significant meaning of that term."[15]

R.B. pointed out that the professor was working with his own definition of *hate* and not with a definition gleaned from the Bible. The following paragraph lays out R.B.'s evaluation.

The Bible tells us that God hated Esau (Mal. 1:3, Rom. 9:13). It also tells us that God loves all men, Esau of course included (Matt. 5:44,45). Dr. Stob tells us that, since God loves all men, he did not really hate Esau. The Bible tells us that God hates certain men (Ps. 11:5). It also tells us that God loves all men. Dr. Stob tells us that, since God loves all men, he does not really hate any. The Bible tells us that God hates wickedness (Ps. 45:7). It also tells us that he hates all workers of iniquity (Ps. 5:5). Dr. Stob tells us that God does indeed hate wickedness but, inasmuch as he loves all men, he does not really hate the workers of iniquity. Just where lies the difficulty? However much one dislikes saying it, it must be said that there is a strain of rationalism in Dr. Stob's interpretation of Scripture. It comes to clear expression in these sentences: "Hate and love are contradictory; they exclude each other. It is logically sound, therefore, to declare that if God hates someone, he does not love him; and if God loves someone, he does not hate him. If it can be established that God hates some men, it will have to be conceded that he does not love all men. Conversely, if it can be established that God loves all men, we are thereby prevented from saying in a truly meaningful way that he hates some of them." That argumentation appears logical. But does not Dr. Stob here employ precisely the same logic as the Reverend Hoeksema is wont to employ? Hoeksema says: "If God hates a person, he does not love him." Stob says in reverse but just as logically: "If God loves a person, he does not hate him." Yet such is not the logic of Scripture. God tells us in his Word that he loves all men and yet hates some. What mortal, pray, has the right to deny that God makes the latter affirmation in a truly meaningfuly way? Whether or not one can fathom its meaning, the fact of God's making it is proof of its meaningfulness.[16]

R.B. concluded his commentary on the professor's writing with this judgment, "In the light of God's self-revelation that he hates all workers of iniquity (Ps. 5:5), Dr. Stob's asseveration that 'to ascribe hate of persons to God is to pervert the very thought of God' stands out as extremely, not to say shockingly, absolutistic."

"De Strijdende Kerk"

R.B. knew something about the struggles of the church. He was very much engaged in many of them. Sometimes when he was so engaged he would use a Dutch expression and say with a sigh, "Het is de strijdende kerk"—it is the church militant. He carried on in the battle for the truth of God's Word from the pulpit not only, but also by his use of the pen and also at the annual sessions of the synod of the church.

One of the more important issues to which R.B. addressed himself at synod was a proposal that the church become involved in a program of united theological education in Nigeria. This matter was before the church for some five years. It began with a decision to lend a missionary to be a teacher for the training of native pastors in Nigeria. That teacher was Dr. Harry Boer. This decision led in time to a request from the Board of Foreign Missions and the Nigerian General Conference (missionaries on the field) that the Christian Reformed Church "*participate* in the program for united theological education in Northern Nigeria" by being involved in the sponsoring and maintaining of the Theological College of Northern Nigeria (usually referred to by the initials TCNN). There was much opposition to this proposal in the church on the ground that such united theological education, with different theological viewpoints represented, would compromise the doctrinal principles of the Christian Reformed Church. The issue brought on a long drawn out debate that was finally concluded in 1959 when the Synod decided that "the Christian Reformed Church *participate in TCNN only to the extent of loaning* Dr. H. Boer as teacher of Reformed Theology in the TCNN."[17] R.B. Kuiper made a significant contribution on the floor of synod to the careful wording of that decision. He was very much opposed to any participation in the united seminary that went beyond loaning a "teacher of Reformed theology" to the school.[18]

The Synod of 1959 was also the setting for a dramatic speech by R.B. Kuiper. In this speech he made plain that in good conscience he had to oppose the appointment of the Professor of Ethics and Apologetics to "an indefinite term." In doing so R.B. was speaking against the reappointment of one of the ablest and most popular professors at the seminary. When he was president of Calvin College R.B. had known the future professor as an able scholar and prominent student leader. As professor at Calvin Seminary he wielded much influence at the school and in the church. He could use the English language masterfully. R.B.'s objection to the man's reappointment did not rise out of personal animosity. About two months before the session of synod R.B. received a cordial note from the professor thanking him for the gift of copies of Kuiper's two latest publications. R.B.'s objection could mean only that he was fully persuaded that the teacher had failed measurably to meet the standards that he had set up for those who would teach at the school of Reformed theology. Earlier in this chapter is evidence of the marked difference in the thinking of these two men. Further indication of such sharp difference is apparent from a careful reading of what each has said on the important subject of the *Antithesis*. Such careful reading reveals the clash between these two leading figures in their views of history's great conflict between the believer and the unbeliever, the regenerate and the unregenerate, between the church and the world, between Christ and Satan.[19] Incidentally, R.B. and the professor were on opposite sides in the debate over the church's role in TCNN.

R.B.'s Dark Moment at Synod

It happened in connection with the discussions at synod on the universal love of God as construed by the Professor of Missions. The Synod of 1963 was the setting. A classis came to the Synod with a request that the professor be asked, under the terms of the Form of Subscription, to give further explanation of his views. The argument went back and forth over the propriety of the overture and especially over the adequacy of its grounds. At one point a member of synod requested that Professor R.B. Kuiper, President Emeritus of Calvin Seminary, be asked whether in his judgment the classis had furnished adequate grounds for its overture. Before R.B. could rise to speak the president of synod gave him sharp warning that he was speaking under restrictions, namely, that he could not enter into any discussion of the professor's views. R.B. responded to the effect that he could not possibly answer the question put to him without some evaluation. So R.B. was not allowed to answer the question put to him. There was applause in the visitor's gallery when R.B.'s voice was stifled. The applause brought rebuke from the chairman. It was a humiliating moment for R.B. Kuiper.

It could be argued that the president of synod could hardly have done otherwise since the general question at issue was whether synod should enter into a discussion and evaluation of the professor's views. On the other hand R.B., in his written protest to synod on the treatment he had received, claimed that some evaluation was needed to answer the question put to him because the precise question being debated was the adequacy of the grounds of the overture. There was considerable criticism of the peremptory manner in which the president of synod dealt with the respected elder churchman. In his protest R.B. asked that his communication be included in the Acts of Synod. The president assured him that it would be, along with notice of the fact that the protest was not sustained on appeal. The next morning, at the reading of the previous day's minutes, the president declared that nothing of this would be entered in the record.[20] R.B. Kuiper never again appeared at a session of the synod of the Christian Reformed Church.

Dedication of the Centennial Seminary

It was a happier occasion when R.B. delivered the key address at the dedication of the new Centennial Memorial Calvin Seminary building. The new structure was erected on the recently purchased Knollcrest Campus, a beautiful wooded tract obtained by the Christian Reformed Church for Calvin College and Seminary in 1956. R.B. had been a member of the Long-Range Planning Committee that recommended the purchase of the spacious site.

The dedication, which took place in the spring of 1961, was a notable occasion for R.B. Kuiper for a number of reasons. This was the third seminary building in whose dedication he was involved. In 1893, as observed in an earlier chapter, R.B. at the age of seven accompanied his father at the dedication of the new home of the Theological School at the corner of Franklin Street and what was later named Madison Avenue. Then when R.B. was president of Calvin College in the early thirties he brought greetings from the college at the time of the dedication of the Hekman Memorial seminary building on the Franklin Street campus. So a good bit of personal history was in the making when R.B. gave the dedicatory address at the Knollcrest Campus in 1961.

His address was a typical R.B. Kuiper production, with an intriguing title and a clear, timely thrust. "Change and Decay—Abide and Grow" was the title. The thesis of the speech was that if the seminary should depart from the changeless truth it professes it will decay, but if it abides in that truth it will grow and grow. The speaker specified four *unchangeables* with which the school in God's gracious providence should always abide. These four unchangeables are *God, Jesus Christ, the written word, the way of salvation by God's sovereign grace*. [21]

No Letup

As the years of his life continued to mount there was no lessening of his labors for the truth he loved and the church he served. Articles flowed unchecked from his pen. Considerable time and strength were expended in giving advice to many who sought his good counsel. By letter or personal visit to the Kuiper home they came to consult him about problems in local churches or about issues in the church at large. Consistory members came to get his advice concerning possible candidates to pastor their churches. Even seminary students came to talk to him about matters on which there were differences of opinion at the school.

A unique contribution to discussions on church, theology and related matters brought out R.B.'s ripe insights in crisply clear fashion. A group led by businessman Adrian De Vos of Grand Haven put out some sight-sound productions which had the format of a dialogue with R.B. as the interviewee. One of these, captioned *Modern Tower of Babel*, discussed humanism as it has come to expression in the world and as it has also invaded the church. Under the heading *A Shorn Samson* another production dealt with the danger that the church become flabby and ineffective due to neglect or weakening of the biblical teachings on which God's house is founded.[22]

Westminster Seminary called on him in 1963 to deliver the commencement address one more time, the last of several such occasions. He spoke on the subject "The Corruption of the Best." The theme came from the old Latin expression *Corruptio optimi pessima*, which means "The corruption of the best is the worst." In the speech with its arresting title he dwelt on the tactics used by Satan in corrupting the best.

> What are his tactics when he operates as an angel of light? Of his many devices let me specify two. Often he mingles a little truth with a big lie. In that way he would render the lie palatable. However, if I may change the metaphor, that is hardly his trump card. Perhaps his cleverest device is to mingle a little lie with a big truth. Often the lie is so small in comparison with the truth as to be hardly noticeable. In other words, he leavens the most precious truths of the Christian religion with just a bit of falsehood. But when that leaven has done its work the result is appalling. The corruption of the best has become the worst.[23]

The larger portion of R.B.'s address was taken up by illustrations of the devil's use of his "trump card." Several of these dealt with ways in which the infallibility of Scripture was proclaimed by many, even some "self-styled conservatives," but that infallibility is then limited to matters of faith and morals or to the *kerugma*, and not equally applied to items deemed to be peripheral.

His Last Sermon

As R.B. continued to spend himself for his first love, Christ's church and kingdom, it was gradually becoming apparent that his physical resources were beginning to give way. This was an almost imperceptible process, until May 10, 1964. On that day he was preaching in one of his former charges, the West Leonard Street Christian Reformed Church. It was the morning worship service, the first of two he was to conduct that day. His text was Psalm 86:10—"For thou art great, and doest wondrous things: thou alone art God." His theme was "The Only True God." That was material for a great sermon by R.B. Kuiper. About half way through his sermon the always eloquent preacher stumbled in his speech. As the hushed audience looked on with concern he hesitated, tried to go on, but could not. He indicated that he was unable to recover his train of thought and he had to quit. The vice-president of the consistory took over, read a poem he had in his pocket and dismissed the congregation. Thus the long distinguished service of this extraordinarily gifted pulpiteer came to a halt.

Early in 1965 another episode took its toll of his waning strength. He was hospitalized for ten days due to prostate surgery. After that he gradually began to lose his appetite for food. He had always been a hearty eater. He made light of his lack of interest in food, making jokes about his new-found interest in the slendering fad. He did this for Mrs. Kuiper's sake, as he did not want her to worry about him. Since their marriage he had been her number one concern.

His Last Book

His ebbing strength was not reflected in a weakening of his resolve to keep on working for the cause he loved. The pulpit and the rostrum were now closed to him, but he could still wield the pen. He was working on a book which quite appropriately expressed his will to write for the edification of those who filled the pews in the churches. The appealing title he had chosen was *The Bible Tells Us So*. One can hardly fail to recognize that the title was suggested by the words of a familiar children's hymn, "Jesus loves me, this I know, for the Bible tells me so." The book offers "popular presentations of basic teachings of the Christian religion over against current distortions and denials." The author's "appeal throughout is not to the speculations of philosophers, or for that matter of theologians, but to Holy Scripture" (Introduction).[24] R.B. very much wanted to complete this piece of work and he hoped that death would not thwart his strong desire. But God ruled otherwise. Yet, though the book, published posthumously, was not completed, it did reach a large host of readers, among them many in the Orient, as the book was translated into the Chinese language.

In the early morning hours of April 22, 1966 this valiant soldier of Jesus Christ breathed his last. His stout heart failed. His daughter and son were at his side. We who were close to him and loved him have missed his stimulating presence very much. Perhaps the church, to which he spoke so clearly for more than half a century, has missed him too.

Chapter 19

The Legacy of R.B. Kuiper

The foregoing chapters of this book have left with the reader impressions of R.B. Kuiper that are quite inescapable. There is no need to present a recital of those impressions now. There are, however, some elements in the record he left that deserve some elaboration.

He left a legacy that has a strong personal character. Among his contemporaries the familiar initials "R.B." were sometimes rendered by the words "rare bird." Such he was. It was said of him that he simply could not be typed; he did not fit any common mold. The editor of a church paper saw in those initials the words "rijk begaafd," meaning richly endowed. His was a rich personality. His conversation and wit glistened. His public speech was commanding, his logic compelling, his sense of the biblical message most persuasive, his performance in church councils enlightening and sometimes formidable. And there was always a sparkle in his eye—a sparkle of warm goodwill, a sparkle accompanying animated discourse, or a gleam of intensity as he preached, especially when his subject was the glorious salvation we have by God's matchless grace in Christ Jesus.

R.B. was a man whom to have known was an enriching experience. Such "rare birds" are indeed rare. One person, a member of a congregation pastored by R.B., sensed this when he sent him a card inscribed with these words, "To a man on a man's birthday." Though a memoir written about this man must fall immeasurably far short of imparting an adequate awareness of this person, it would be regrettable if some portrait of this remarkable man of God were not left to bless God's children who come after him. This book is an effort to convey the strong personal quality of his legacy so that the hearts of many may be gripped with a sense of the vitality and intensity that charged the life and labors of R.B. Kuiper.

Sentient insight into the personality of R.B. Kuiper is furnished by a former student. Coming from a background quite different from that which bred R.B. and not knowing anything whatsoever about the man until he sat in his classroom at Westminster, the student has given the following sensitive description of his first impressions of his professor.

> Two things I remember especially about him, very brief fleeting instances. One was in preaching class as RB was reciting George Herbert's lines, "Teach me, my God and King, in all things Thee to see, And what I do in any thing I do it as for Thee." I think that's the way the lines go. But I remember having the impression as RB quoted the lines that his voice went soft and his eyes moistened. I thought, "This guy is genuine. He's not just getting off a quote; he feels it, he believes it, it's the way he wants his life to be even tho he is a very strong logical theologian." Maybe I imagined it. Maybe I wasn't seeing well. Maybe it was the light in the room. But I've thought about it. And then one day RB was telling us how to recite a line with force, with passion, with understanding, so as to open up the power of the words to listeners, not just mouth them (the words). This time it was "Love so amazing, so divine, demands my soul, my life, my all." And again I thought his voice quivered, his eyes went moist, and again I thought, "This man believes it. He'd give his life. He's ready to go all the way." Well, so it was for me with RB, little things, brief moments, that have always been with me.[1]

Another former student, in speaking of the place that Professor R.B. Kuiper had taken in his life, said in words carrying much warmth that next to his father R.B. had been the most commanding personality to influence his life.

The Preacher

He had to preach. His father's strong influence, his rearing, his grace-given commitment to Jesus Christ, the capture of his mind and heart by the teaching of Scripture, the gifts God gave him—all these together led him to the pulpit. R.B. Kuiper could say with the apostle Paul, "Yet when I preach the gospel, I cannot boast, for I am compelled to preach. Woe to me if I do not preach the gospel" (I Cor. 9:16). Salvation by the wondrous sovereign grace of God in Christ Jesus was the light of his life which lit fires in his soul and put a bright gleam in his eye. This gospel he had to preach and he did it with joy and with power.

Thousands heard him preach and they were thrilled, they were instructed and they were inspired. This prince of the pulpit touched the lives of so many. He received many letters from people who heard him preach and had been blessed by his message. He rekindled the faith of many. He warmed the hearts of many. He helped many see the glory of Christianity. These blessings are an enduring legacy in the lives of so many who heard him.

The heritage left to the church by R.B. Kuiper the preacher lives on in the ministry of the many students who sat under his teaching. What he imparted to them was not simply a body of teaching about sermonizing and ministry that was passed on from previous generations. His teaching reflected thorough knowledge of such a corpus of homiletical instruction. But what he taught was much more than that. He taught his students those principles and insights which were first of all biblical, and which had informed and inspired his own highly successful ministry of the Word of God.

Nor did R.B. pass on to his students a syllabus on the techniques of pulpit performance, as he saw in the chapter on "Teacher of Preachers." He taught them the *principles* that should guide and govern their ministry, especially the two principles of *Scriptura Sola* and *Scriptura Tota*. There were other important principles, and how pertinent they were. He summarized many of these guidelines in a paragraph in one of his later books. In this book he named a number of able pulpiteers (some of whom he disagreed with theologically) who, he said, "were easy to listen to, could grip and hold an audience, knew how to put a message across." Compared to their pulpit work, R.B. said that much preaching is "insufferably dull." Then he produced a paragraph that every aspiring preacher and active preacher should read.

The practical is more interesting than the theoretical. Therefore every doctrinal sermon should be made intensely vital. That holds even of a sermon on the Trinity or the divine decrees. The concrete is more interesting than the abstract. For that reason illustrations are useful. One reason, no doubt, why the common people heard the Lord Jesus gladly (Mark 12:37) was that His parables made His teaching outstandingly concrete. The advice is still good that the preacher should turn the ears of his listeners into eyes. The contemporaneous is particularly interesting. Audiences are more concerned about the new orthodoxy than about the Socinianism of the sixteenth and seventeenth centuries. Lucidity of thought and expression are more interesting than are unfamiliar words and complicated sentences. The apostle Paul said he would rather speak five easily understood words than ten thousand in an unknown tongue (I Cor. 14:19). Freshness of expression, short of straining for originality and with due recognition of established doctrinal vocabulary, is more interesting than are clichés and hackneyed terminology. The latter have a way of putting people to sleep. Flowery language may become nauseating. Repetitiousness is usually the result of inadequate preparation and can only result in loss of attention. Mispronunciations and errors in grammar are not only uninteresting, but displeasing as well, for the simple reason that the ugly offends the sensibilities. A pompous delivery is disgusting because it suggests insincerity. On the other hand, a simple and conversational, yet forceful, delivery commands both respect and response. Enthusiasm inspires. Logic is convincing, the illogical confusing. As preachers let us have a heart. Let us stop wearying our audiences. Let us make our preaching so absorbingly interesting that even the children will rather listen to us than draw pictures and will thus put to shame their paper-and-pencil-supplying parents. But we may as well make up our minds that an absolute prerequisite of such preaching is the most painstaking preparation.[2]

After one has digested the chapter entitled "Teacher of Preachers" and has read the above quotation he greets with a great deal of interest a recent evaluation of Professor Kuiper's work as teacher of Homiletics. Dr. Carl E. Zylstra sees his preaching and work in Homiletics as a "fresh breeze" sweeping through an era in the Christian Reformed Church between the years 1935 and 1975. R.B.'s preaching is described as "direct, clear, concrete and lively." Regarding his work in Homiletics Zylstra observes that R.B. held tenaciously to his Calvinistic principles but "opened up the possibility of adaptability in concepts and flexibility in practice." However, he concludes that R.B.'s significance appears to be more in the realm of potential rather than actual influence."

Zylstra's concern in his dissertation is with the Christian Reformed Church and its experience in adjusting to American culture in the years 1935 to 1975. This colors his evaluation of R.B. Kuiper's work in Homiletics, which was done almost wholly at Westminster Seminary and affected mainly churches other than the Christian Reformed, especially the Orthodox Presbyterian Church. Students taught by R.B. must bear this fact in mind as they assess Zylstra's otherwise astonishing judgment that R.B.'s significance lay more in the realm of potential rather than actual influence. This judgment by Zylstra must also be seen in connection with his observation that R.B. "never really systematized his approach," meaning, it would appear, that he never authored a book on Homiletics. If the judgment means that R.B.'s instruction in Homiletics was not systematized, his students would have to demur. These students will wonder how well Zylstra knew either R.B. Kuiper or Westminster Theological Seminary when he says that R.B.'s "heavy person-oriented emphasis in practice tended to get lost in the intellectualistic atmosphere of Westminster."[3]

Of singular importance in the homiletical equation is another factor that must be borne in mind in any evaluation of R.B. Kuiper's performance as a practitioner and teacher of Homiletics. I refer to the person of the preacher himself. Preaching is a highly personalized business. The personality of the preacher with his particular background, gifts, psychological makeup and moral character has a tremendous bearing on his work in the pulpit and on his ministry generally. This factor was of great significance to R.B. Kuiper. He insisted that every preacher be himself in proclaiming the Word under the rule of the principles and guidelines that he sought to impart to his students. R.B. is the best illustration of the role of the preacher's personality in sermonizing. Take away the gifts and personality traits that he had and what is left of the preaching of R.B. Kuiper? It was his personal uniqueness that contributed greatly to the effectiveness and success of his ministry of the Word. The freedom to be himself was an insistent priority with him. At the same time he was just as insistent in urging that every preacher treasure and exercise this authentic personal freedom in the pulpit. He was not at all interested in having his students become his clones. So he urged the future preachers to make use of the model of the "ideal homily" in the pulpit, but he did not insist on a wooden, rigid use of the model. He allowed for variations in application according to the preacher's judicious preference, so long as the Word of God was faithfully and effectively proclaimed. According to the Bible God is pleased to build His church and kingdom especially through the preaching of His Word by human beings with all the varieties of gifts and character with which He has equipped them. This key personal factor sets limits to systematization in Homiletics.

The Theologian

R.B. Kuiper was an able preacher who was also an able theologian. If he had not been that he would not have been true to the home from which he came. Also, we have seen that he insisted that Practical Theology, the branch of seminary instruction he taught for many years, is *theology*. But he was not what most people regard as a typical academic theologian, a person given to expressing himself in language that seems abstruse to the average person. This hallmark of R.B. Kuiper's writing, teaching and public speaking is described aptly by Professor John Murray in his Foreword to R.B.'s last publication *The Bible Tells Us So*. "His writing, as his preaching and lecturing," wrote Professor Murray, "was always characterized by clarity and simplicity. Obscurity of expression never marred his written or spoken word. This was the fruit of chastened scholarship, so much so that we are liable to overlook the mature thought behind it. Kuiper never made a pretense of erudition; such pretense he abhorred. But erudition of the truest hue there was, and the discerning could discover it in his penetrating and perspicuous analyses."[4]

Three adjectives best describe the thinking of preacher-theologian R.B. Kuiper. These three terms are Scriptural, Reformed and Balanced. We deal briefly with each.

Scriptural

In life's whirlwind of change and human fumbling there is one visible and tangible reality that gives stability and direction to man's existence. This was the case in the life and ministry of R.B. Kuiper. At every point his life and labor bore witness to the supreme place of the Scriptures, the Scriptures being the very Word, the infallible and inerrant Word, of the living God. This testimony of R.B.'s life appears in the title of the book he wrote as the end of his days on earth approached. *The Bible Tells Us So* is the eloquently simple language of R.B.'s witness to the truth that to him was changeless and sure. And what the Bible tells us first of all is that "The Bible Is God's Word," the heading of the first chapter of the book.

In his preaching he was always deeply conscious of being *Verbi Divini Minister*—a servant of the divine Word. He taught his students that this is what they should aspire to be, and nothing less or other than that. Above all else preaching had to be scriptural, always based on thorough exegesis of the Bible and always imparting the biblical message. And study of the Bible produced something akin to the poison of asps if that study was carried out in such a manner that human judgment was somehow placed above the sovereign instruction of that Word. R.B. agreed wholeheartedly with some advice his colleague J. Gresham Machen gave to the students. Machen warned them that no matter how learned or impressive some professor or preacher might sound, his teaching should be held suspect if a high view of the Bible as God's very Word did not come through with unmistakable clarity. The so-called "new hermeneutic" was coming on the scene in the latter years of R.B.'s life. He saw its potential for evil as a sophisticated new tool for Bible study that could very readily place human judgment above the Word of the sovereign God. So he stressed the timelessness and the timeliness of the Word.

Reformed

One person said R.B. Kuiper was Reformed from the top of his head to the soles on his feet. Another said he was Reformed to the marrow of his bones. Even a casual reading of R.B.'s writings bears out the aptness of such remarks. For him it was false to speak of the Reformed or Calvinistic faith as being something added to or in any way superimposed on the Scriptures. Like a brightly colored cord there runs a line of thinking through all his writing and speaking that maintains that the teaching of the Bible and the teaching of the Reformed faith are virtually identical, that Calvinism is Christianity in its truest and purest form, that the Reformed faith is the faith of the Bible. He never withdrew in any way or in any circumstance from that position and he never apologized for it, not even faintly so. He was surprised when some members of the Christian Reformed Church criticized Rev. Peter Eldersveld for preaching a series of sermons on the five points of Calvinism on the Back-To-God Hour, radio voice of the denomination. R.B. applauded Eldersveld's choice of material for sermons preached to his large mixed radio audience. After all, in preaching thus Eldersveld was simply preaching Christianity, the very heart of Christianity, that is, salvation by God's grace.

It must be noted that for R.B. the Reformed faith or Calvinism included more, much more, than the so-called five points of Calvinism, namely, Total Depravity, Unconditional Election, Limited Atonement, Irresistible Grace and Perseverance of the Saints. These five points form the very core of the faith, R.B. insisted, in that they teach salvation by God's sovereign and efficacious grace. This was the great good news that R.B. felt constrained to preach and how he loved to preach it. But Calvinism includes more. R.B. stressed that the faith also includes important teachings like the infallibility of the Bible, the Covenant of Grace, the free and sincere offer of the gospel to all people, the Lordship of Jesus Christ over all of life, the claims of general revelation in its relationship to special revelation, and the many-faceted subject of the church as the body of Christ.

Was R.B. narrowly parochial in making these high claims

for the Reformed faith? Was there a touch of arrogance or triumphalism in his claims? There were those who thought so. Yet, can anyone who confesses the Reformed creeds say anything less than what R.B. said? In the Christian Reformed Church every elder, deacon, preacher and professor at Calvin College and Seminary solemnly signs a Form of Subscription in which the signatory avows that the teachings of the Confession of Faith, the Heidelberg Catechism and the Canons of Dort "do fully agree with the Word of God." Presbyterians who subscribe to the Calvinistic Westminster Standards make a similar avowal. Can any such signatory then allow that conflicting interpretations of the Word of God also "fully agree" with the Bible's teaching?

A recent book entitled *Christian and Reformed Today* written by John Bolt comments on these high claims of R.B. Kuiper (and Warfield) for the Reformed faith. While lamenting and rejecting any pride or smugness that such claims might be in danger of carrying, Bolt says, "I also wonder if the reason for the relative absence of claims such as that of Kuiper and Warfield is that many Reformed people no longer know or value their own tradition. Many Christians simply view the plethora of ecclesial traditions and church denominations as a kind of smorgasbord in which personal preference and taste are the order of the day. Concern about the truth of doctrine or confession seems waning. If Christians no longer value their own tradition, often because they do not know its true genius, they cannot be convinced of its being the purest and truest expression of Christianity."[5] To the question why they believe as they do many Christians are satisfied to reply that "it's the group into which I was born," according to Bolt.

Triumphalism was not present in R.B.'s high claims for the Reformed faith. He did not regard Calvinism in the way in which a high school or college cheerleader looks at her favorite team. It was simply his straightforward and well-nourished conviction that the Reformed faith in all its richness is the teaching of the Bible. At the same time he was always ready to accept as a brother or sister in Christ anyone who loved the Scriptures and named the name of Jesus Christ as Savior and Lord, without in any way compromising his Calvinistic stance. Those who demur at these high claims for the Reformed faith would do well to take a look at the third volume of Philip Schaff's valuable work *The Creeds of Christendom*. One is struck by the large number of creedal statements that gave expression to the teachings of John Calvin as compared with the far fewer such statements of faith appearing in other branches of Protestantism. The Spirit of truth that Christ promised His followers appears to have been especially active in the Reformed family of churches.

Balanced

When R.B. used the words *balance* or *balanced* in his writings he was not referring first of all to emotional and intellectual stability that avoids extreme or fanatical positions, although he felt that an authentic commitment to Calvinism does indeed guard against such positions. The word balance(d) takes on a more commanding place in R.B.'s thought. In fact, the word represents an important key in his understanding of the truth as revealed in God's Word. Because the word balance(d) does not have an academic flavoring, its significance can easily be overlooked.

R.B. taught that there are in scriptural teaching paradoxes that do not bow to human logic. In using the term *paradox* R.B. was referring to *complementary truths* that man's logic or reason sees as contradictory. For believers the truth lies in a hearty acceptance of such paradoxes involving complementary truths. Truth seen in this light is thus balanced. No facet of divine revelation is slighted as justice is done to all aspects of seemingly contradictory truths, and we are in a position to avoid the ever present pitfalls of extremism, rationalism or heresy. So important was this view of biblical truth to R.B. that he declared that it "may be said to be the acid test of Calvinism," which involves "a willingness to accept unreservedly the paradoxes of Holy Scripure."[6]

Some of the complementary truths which R.B. saw as the teaching of the Bible are the following:

Divine Sovereignty   —   Human Responsibility
Election   —   The Covenant of Grace

Reprobation	—	The Sincere Universal Offer of the Gospel
Antithesis	—	Common Grace
Christ's Deity	—	Christ's Humanity
Scriptural Particularism	—	Scriptural Universalism
God Loves All Men	—	God Hates Some Men

"The Reformed theology," wrote R.B., "is not a closed system every part of which according to the laws of human logic fits in perfectly with every other part. Contrariwise, when the Calvinist is completely certain that a matter is taught in the Word of God, he takes that matter into his system, whether it seems to fit in or not. For him the test of truth is not human reason but the Word of God. He willingly subjects human logic to the divine *logos*." This is what is meant by saying that "the Reformed faith embraces 'the whole counsel of God' (Acts 20:27)."[7] His demonstrated unswerving loyalty to "the whole counsel of God" is no small part of the legacy R.B. Kuiper left behind.

The Churchman

The church, the church, the church—what a large place it filled in the life of R.B. Kuiper. He was always so very much involved with all matters pertaining to the church. His high view of the importance of the church was not limited to the ideal church, sometimes called the invisible church. He meant also the church as we see it and know it, with all of its checkered history and its present foibles.

Early in his career he wrote affectionately about the church in an article entitled "Why I Love My Mother." We take note of some of what he said.

The Christian Reformed Church is my mother.

She hasn't been feeling any too well for some time. Just lately she is having a pretty bad case of the blues.

It's the boys that are worrying her.

Several of them are engaged in a dispute. You might suppose that she would be accustomed to that by this time. Well, perhaps she is. Fact is, she doesn't mind at all if they carry on a lusty debate so long as they behave well. She rather enjoys it. But just now they are going pretty far. Several times she has

overheard insulting remarks. Nasty insinuations abound. She
fears the boys don't love each other as brothers should.[8]

This article appeared in 1922 just when the celebrated Janssen
controversy was reaching its climax.

Although R.B. always had a special feeling for his mother
church, his vision was not limited to one denomination. When
he named his book on the church *The Glorious Body of Christ*,
he said he wasn't thinking of any one denomination. He served
in three different denominations. His ease in moving about
among the various churches came from a confidence that he
could serve his Lord and preach the Word faithfully in these different ecclesiastical settings. It will be recalled that he said that
he would not have been the least bit interested in the presidency
of Calvin College if it were not squarely based on the Reformed
faith. That was his true love. He honored ecclesiastical institutions, but he did not worship them. He worshipped only the God
of truth, and he could be happy serving in a denomination so
long as he felt that church strove to be "pillar and ground of the
truth" (I Tim. 3:15). This above all was the reason why he called
the church the *glorious* body of Christ, for "that glory shines
forth resplendently from God's infallible Word."[9]

As churchman R.B. was an alert and faithful watchman on
the walls of Zion. Some pastors are content to spend themselves
in the steadfast preaching of God's Word and tending the flock
God has entrusted to them. Thoroughly commendable as such
pastoring is, it was not to be R.B.'s ministry. His rich gifts, soon
recognized by the church, didn't allow for such a ministry. And
he was filled with zeal for the truth of the Word. The faith was
too precious to him that he could ignore departures from it.
Also, a confessional commitment once made had to be honored.
Therefore he spoke out frequently against views which he was
convinced were unbiblical and contrary to the confession of the
church.

Consequently he had little patience with church leaders who
did not speak out on issues in the church when occasion clearly
called for men to take a stand. Such leaders might enjoy a
reputation as faithful pastors, but for some reason they refrain
from fighting the battles of the Lord in the councils of the
church. Such leaders often hold to the middle of the road and

are quite ready to move either way on an issue, depending on prevailing winds of opinion in the church. R.B. detested such behavior. Such behavior is often in the interest of peace in the church, a state desirable to all. But any behavior that sought peace at the expense of truth was anathema to R.B., not because he loved controversy but because he dearly loved the truth he and the church confessed. His record of faithfulness as a watchman on the walls of Zion is also part of a legacy that the church ought to treasure.

R.B.'s Vision

After R.B. had served in a second denomination he wrote a piece called "A Vision." It is the last chapter of his book *As To Being Reformed* (1926). Following is some of it.

> And it shall come to pass that the truly Reformed Christians of this continent, scattered throughout various denominations, will be gathered together into one body: *The American Reformed Church* . . . .
> And upon the realization of the noble project, the members of this church will kneel in humble adoration and exclaim: "What hath God wrought!" . . .
> While at first its growth will be slow because of that traditionalism which is common to all men, eventually its branches will reach every corner of this vast land, and the children of God of Reformed persuasion everywhere will sit in its shade.
> The Confessions of this church will embody all the salient truths of the Reformed Standards of former centuries, with additions as the Holy Spirit may direct and the exigencies of the age require.
> The principle underlying its government in every manifestation will be the Kingship of Jesus Christ.
> The tolerance of Christ will be practised in this church: the constituent bodies will not trouble one another because of differences due to sectional traits and traditions.

Thirty-three years later he recalled the vision. This time he broadened it to include all "self-consciously Reformed Christians . . . *throughout* the world." They should be striving for "one form or another of organic union."[10] He spoke favorably of the Reformed Ecumenical Synod, founded in 1949, and hoped it might prove to be a first step toward attaining his global vision.

A vision is just that—a vision. Translation of a vision into reality is quite another matter. Since R.B. wrote significant changes have occurred in the Reformed family of churches. The Christian Reformed Church is less of a homogeneous group than it once was. Important developments, some of them disheartening, continue to occur in the Reformed churches in The Netherlands. Realignment of denominational boundaries among self-consciously Reformed believers in the Presbyterian family of churches in America together with the birth and rapid growth of the Presbyterian Church in America are matters worthy of note. At the same time serious tensions have developed in the Reformed Ecumenical Synod. But may any Reformed Christian call R.B.'s vision mere fantasy? The day may yet come when his vision will become reality, and the church will recall this aspect of R.B.'s legacy.

As preacher he wanted to be only *Verbi Divini Minister*—servant of the divine Word. As theologian he wholeheartedly embraced and promoted the Reformed faith because it was eminently scriptural. As churchman he fought valiantly in the councils of the church and elsewhere that the truth of the Word might prevail. He was like the prophets of the Bible, whose calling was to bring the Word of God, nothing more, nothing less. When R.B. was here the church knew there was a prophet in the land. May he yet speak and be heard.

Notes

Chapter 1

1. When the author of this book was a growing boy in northwestern Iowa he still heard the word *Afgescheiden* as an expression of approbrium in name-calling.

2. The Dutch title is *Het modernisme, een Fata Morgana op christelijk gebied*.

3. A sizable portion of the Christian Reformed Church did not join in the union forged in 1892. So that church remains part of the ecclesiastical scene in Holland.

Chapter 2

1. The Dutch title as given by the translator E.R. Post was *Eene Stem uit America over America*.

2. The Kuipers did not stop at Ellis Island, which began to serve as a place for the processing of immigrants in 1892, one year after the Kuipers arrived.

3. From address given October 1945 before the Midwest Christian Teachers' Association. Subject of the address was "The Influence of our Christian Schools on America."

4. *De Wachter*, Oct. 20, 1919.

5. *Uit Eigen Kring* (Out of Our Own Circle). J.B. Hulst, Grand Rapids.

6. *Yearbook of the Christian Schools of America 1925-26*, p. 94.

7. *Ibid.*

8. Sermon appeared in *De Gereformeerde Amerikaan*, Feb. 1907, pp. 71ff.

9. See John A. Vander Ark, "The Christian School Movement" in *One Hundred Years in the New World*, centennial publication of the Christian Reformed Church, p. 141.

10. Timmerman, *Promises to Keep*, 1975, p. 24. See also article "A Growing Calvin College" by Professors Strikwerda and Timmerman in *One Hundred Years in the New World*, pp. 79ff.

11. *De Wachter*, March 23, 1921.

12. This significant little book by B.K. Kuiper is discussed appreciatively and at some length in Timmerman's *Promises To Keep*, pp. 35-38.

Chapter 3

1. Fiftieth Anniversary 1891-1941 booklet of the school, p. 41.
2. *Ibid.*, p. 12.
3. Address before Midwest Christian Teachers' Association, October 1945.
4. When R.B. Kuiper entered Van Vlissingen school his brother Barend, having received the A.B. degree from the University of Chicago, began teaching in the Literary Department of the Theological School in Grand Rapids at the age of twenty-two.
5. The absorbing story of Wm. Rainey Harper and the University of Chicago is told in *The University of Chicago Magazine*, Part II, June 1941. Here we learn that at the age of three little Willie Harper, sitting in church on a hot day with his parents, walked calmly down the aisle during the service to ask for a drink of water when he saw the minister take a drink from the glass reserved for him.

Chapter 4

1. The year before R.B. entered the Theological School, Peter A. Hoekstra enrolled as the first student to enter the school with an A.B. degree. He had received the degree from the University of Chicago, where he and R.B. had been classmates.
2. In 1908 the Christian Reformed Church adopted the so-called Conclusion of Utrecht. The first of these four "Conclusions" deals with the supra-infra matter. See Schaver, *The Polity of the Churches*, Vol. 2, pp. 34-37.
3. The interested reader can pursue the Supralapsarianism vs. Infralapsarianism question by consulting Berkhof's *Systematic Theology*, pp. 118-125; or Boettner's *The Reformed Doctrine of Predestination*, pp. 126-130 (both volumes 4th ed.).
4. G.D. De Jong, writing in the *Semi-Centennial Volume Theological School and Calvin College*, 1926, p. 39.
5. The name of the Theological School and the college in Grand Rapids was changed to Calvin College and Seminary in 1930.
6. In 1934 the Synod rejected an overture with the following terse dictum as one of two grounds: "It is not correct to say that the so-called principle of 'Free Study' is among us as an officially accepted Reformed principle."
7. IS JESUS GOD—An argument by graduates of Princeton Seminary. American Tract Society, New York, 1912. Citation from Kuiper's essay is found on pp. 9f. Among the other contributors were G. Hoeksema and H.H. Meeter.
8. *Semi-Centennial Volume Theological School and Calvin College*, 1926, pp. 40f.

Chapter 5

1. *De Wachter*, July 31, 1912.
2. *Manifold Grace*, Grand Rapids, Eerdmans-Sevensma, 1914, p. 103.
3. *Christian Liberty*, Grand Rapids, Eerdmans-Sevensma, 1914, p. 5.
4. *Christian Liberty*, pp. 23ff.

5. See Footnote (1).

6. In Seventy-fifth Anniversary booklet, 1964.

Chapter 6

1. The congregation's semi-centennial volume 1907-1957.

2. The letter, dated June 15, 1934, was mailed from Jackson, Mississippi, where R.B. spoke at a Bible conference.

3. WTBT, p. 14.

4. WTBT, p. 15.

5. WTBT, p. 16.

6. WTBT, p. 109.

7. WTBT, p. 192. For R.B. Kuiper's later thinking on this matter see the chapter on "The Church and Ecumenism" in *To Be or Not To Be Reformed*, 1959.

8. WTBT, p. 204.

9. WTBT, p. 214.

10. WTBT, pp. 123ff.

Chapter 7

1. See G.D. De Jong's article on the history of the Theological School in the *Semi-Centennial Volume*, 1926, pp. 36-37. Rev. De Jong taught in the school 1908-1914.

2. In 1930 the name of the twin institutions in Grand Rapids became Calvin College and Seminary, as stated earlier.

3. With the appointments made in 1914 the faculty was as follows: Dogmatics, F.M. Ten Hoor; New Testament, L. Berkhof; Old Testament, R. Janssen; Church History, S. Volbeda; Practical Theology, W. Heyns.

4. R.B. Kuiper's description of what happened helps to explain this surprising action of the Synod. "The motion was before the house to disapprove of the action of Janssen's colleagues in bringing their suspicions to the attention of Curatorium before seeing him personally. It seemed that this motion would prevail. Then a good brother suggested that this point be dropped because of its personal implication. He did not like the idea of Synod's virtually rebuking our professors of theology. Thereupon the motion was voted down. But surely one does not need to take a university course in logic to see that not to decide that a thing should have been done is not necessarily equivalent to deciding that it need not have been done." *As To Being Reformed*, pp. 48-49. R.B. was a delegate to the Synod.

5. Janssen frequently expressed his hurt at the failure of his accusers to come to see him.

6. These pamphlets, written in the Holland language, therefore bear these titles: "De Crisis in de Christelijke Gereformeerde Kerk in Amerika" and "Waar Het in de Zaak Janssen Om Gaat."

7. Following are sample items in the student notes that were featured in the controversy:

Item 1: "Whence came the creation-story? Two possibilities: (1) it was given in toto by revelation; (2) by reflection. The former is of little value, for it was revealed to the Patriarchs, it had become so polluted with polytheistic elements that revelation had to cleanse it once more later. Further, it is too mechanical to be acceptable. The second is not unreasonable. It is not unreasonable to think that the first inhabitants led by the Spirit, should by reflection and speculation come to a view of creation. We have an analogy in the Evolutionary system. Evolution, too, is purely speculative when it goes back to the origin. The fact that they constantly hammer away at Gen. 1 shows that they see in it a certain scientific value. This seems to indicate that the story of Gen. 1 is not contradictory to what the human mind can devise." *Acta der Synode 1922*, pp. 128f.

Item 2: Respecting Abraham, "Nowhere in his whole life, is any mention made of the hereafter. If this was absent, we conclude that a deeply religious life and high morality is possible without being anxiously concerned about the life hereafter. Such an intense religious life as that of Abraham did not give room for such thoughts of immortality. And although the N.T. has an essential element of thought on the hereafter and immortality, still even at present one's thoughts are mainly taken up with the present religion. If we live a full Christian life we need not concern ourselves about future life." Janssen's critics compared this with Heb. 11:9-16. *Acta der Synode 1922*, p. 133.

Item 3: "Why is David forbidden to rear temple? Prophets are very conservative. Prophet says that from earliest times Jehovah lived in a tent. Harps back to Mosaic customs. Prophets want to perpetuate Mosaic forms of worship. But David wants a temple. But building must be postponed; looks like compromise. David is out and out progressive. He wants new things providing they pertain to nonessentials." *Acta der Synode 1922*, p. 130.

8. These letters appear in Janssen's *De Synodale Conclusies*, 1923, pp. 3ff.

9. From a thorough and helpful student paper *The Janssen Case in Retrospect* written by James Y. Van Dyk in 1964, p. 21.

10. Every minister, elder and deacon in the Christian Reformed Church and every professor at Calvin College and Seminary signs the so-called Form of Subscription. This subscription means that the signatories declare their agreement with the teachings of the doctrinal standards of the church. "And further, if at any time the Consistory, Classis or Synod, upon sufficient grounds of suspicion and to preserve the uniformity and purity of doctrine, may deem it proper to require of us a further explanation of our sentiments respecting any particular article" of the doctrinal standards, "we do hereby promise to be always willing and ready to comply with such requisition, under the penalty above mentioned . . ." The penalty referred to is suspension from office.

11. *As To Being Reformed*, p. 46.

12. *Acta der Synode 1922*, pp. 177f.

13. See Janssen's pamphlet "The Synodical Judgment and Its Pre-history Examined in the Light of Church Order," Sept. 1922, pp. 42-47 (English translation of title by EH).

14. *Ibid.*, p. 47. Janssen names H. Hoeksema as the one speaking these words. See also R.B. Kuiper's *As To Being Reformed*, pp. 49f.

15. The Dutch name of the movement was Nationale Beweging in de Zaak Janssen.

16. B.K. Kuiper was editor of the influential paper *De Wachter* at the time, a post he left in December of 1922.

17. *As To Being Reformed*, p. 52.

18. See R.B. Kuiper's comments on this fact in *As To Being Reformed*, p. 47.

19. The Janssen case was not the only doctrinal controversy of importance to contribute to R.B.'s education at the time. Dispensationalism as taught by Rev. H. Bultema was condemned by the Synod of 1918. Then, as we have seen, the controversy over Common Grace was heating up while the Janssen case was being dealt with and came to a head in 1924.

20. *The Christian Reformed Church—A Study in Orthodoxy*, 1949, p. 79. J.H. Kromminga, son of D.H. Kromminga, became professor of Historical Theology at Calvin Seminary, and then the school's president for twenty-five years.

Chapter 8

1. ATBR, p. 45.
2. ATBR, pp. 45f.
3. ATBR, pp. 15ff.
4. ATBR, p. 25.
5. ATBR, p. 28.
6. ATBR, preface.
7. ATBR, p. 120.
8. ATBR, pp. 113ff.

Chapter 9

1. From 40th Anniversary booklet, 1927. In 1904 official disapproval of choirs was declared by synod. Article 69 of the Church Order then in force did not mention choirs. In 1926 synod, while discouraging the use of choirs ("except as an aid to congregational singing"), did leave the matter to the discretion of the local consistory. Later rulings clarified the position of the choir in worship services.

2. ATBR, preface. These words are printed in capital letters.

3. *The Banner*, May 20, 1966, p. 8.

4. ATBR, p. 88.

5. *Not of the World*, pp. 22f.

6. NOTW, p. 106.

7. See chapter on "The Church and Its Traditions" in R.B.'s later publication *To Be or Not To Be Reformed*.

8. The writer of these words was Albertus J. Rooks, member of the congregation and for many years associated with Calvin College as Professor of Latin and Dean. The missionary referred to was Dr. Lee S. Huizenga, devoted and highly respected medical missionary to China from 1920 to 1945. Dr. Huizenga's death in China in 1945 came after he suffered serious deterioration of health in an internment camp as prisoner of the Japanese.

9. See Chapter IV on the matter of "free study."

10. *Acta der Synode 1928*, pp. 86ff. As a matter of fact the Synod of 1928 did issue special warning against the three amusements named, very likely because these three had been specified in overtures brought to synod. The history of this whole matter since 1928 suggests that the approach adopted then was only partially effective. The central concern is the individual's spiritual strength and taste which determine what he would see or do, as in the case of movies coming

into the home via television. Let the church enunciate a fine set of biblical principles, as in 1928, and leave their application to the faithful and watchful preaching of the Word of God.

Chapter 10

1. Published by Channel Press, Great Neck, N.Y.c1961.
2. *The Banner*, editorial, May 20, 1966.
3. In a letter dated March 12, 1963, written in response to a letter from R.B. commenting favorably on Eldersveld's radio preaching. Eldersveld's letter has the salutation, Dear Uncle "Bill". He was R.B.'s nephew by marriage.
4. *Calvin College Chimes*, May 6, 1966.
5. In letter to Mrs. Kuiper at the time of her husband's death.
6. Westminster Shorter Catechism, Q-A 1.

Chapter 11

1. R.B.'s Westminster years will be dealt with in following chapters.
2. The address, entitled "The Task of Calvin College," appeared in *The Banner*, No. 65, 1930, pp. 862, 876. Quotations here given are from the original manuscript.
3. John J. Timmerman's book is sub-titled *A Centennial History of Calvin College*.
4. *Promises To Keep*, p. 74.
5. *The Banner*, Feb. 12, 1932.
6. From letter to Mrs. Kuiper at the time of R.B.'s death.
7. *Evangelical Student*, April 1931.

Chapter 12

1. The reorganization at Princeton is a complicated story whose beginning can be pinpointed in the choice of J. Ross Stevenson in 1914 as president. He was more interested in promoting church union than in promoting Calvinism. This story is unfolded in Stonehouse, *J. Gresham Machen—A Biographical Memoir*, 1955.
2. Van Til's appointment had been opposed by Stevenson, who thought of the Christian Reformed Church as a "separatist sect." Stonehouse, *Ibid*, p. 437.
3. *Ibid.*, p. 447.
4. *Ibid.*, p. 171.
5. *Ibid.*, p. 457.
6. *Ibid.*, p. 428.
7. *Ibid.*, p. 457.
8. *The Banner*, Oct. 14, 1932.
9. *The Banner*, April 21, 1933.
10. Adequate discussion of this significant document goes beyond the scope of this book. The reader can profitably consult R.B. Kuiper's article "A Pernicious Document" in *The Banner*, July 5, 1935; and Rian, *The Presbyterian Conflict*, Eerdmans, 1940, pp. 29-59.
11. R.B. Kuiper, *Practical Theology Today* (pamphlet), Westminster Theological Seminary.

12. Machen was affectionately referred to as "Das" (*a* like *o* in deposit) by his friends. This curious appellation was picked up in Machen's student days in Germany. His last name sounded very much like the German word for girl—Mädchen, and the article accompanying this German noun was "das."

Chapter 13

1. Dr. O.T. Allis quickly won the respect of the writer when, in the first course in Old Testament he took with Allis, the professor began with these words, "The Bible begins with a robust theism" (the reference being to Gen. 1:1).

2. Stonehouse, *Ibid.*, p. 140.

3. In *The New Republic*, Jan. 30, 1937. Quoted by Rian, *The Presbyterian Conflict*, p. 216.

4. From "To Our Readers" by the editors in *The Westminster Theological Journal* Vol. I, No. 1, Nov. 1938.

5. A most helpful service has been performed by Peter De Klerk, Theological Librarian of Calvin College and Seminary, in the compilation of *A Bibliography of the Writings of the Professors of Calvin Theological Seminary*, in 1980. The reader can consult this useful volume to learn about R.B. Kuiper's extensive writings.

6. Published by Zondervan in Grand Rapids, 1942. Quotation is from page 3.

7. From Bulletin of Westminster Theological Seminary, Summer 1966.

Chapter 14

1. *As To Being Reformed*, p. 154.

2. *The Infallible Word*. The Presbyterian Guardian Publishing Corp., Philadelphia, 1946, p. 209.

3. *Ibid.*, p. 212.

4. *Ibid.*, pp. 213f.

5. *Ibid.*, pp. 210.

6. *Ibid.*, p. 228.

7. *Ibid.*, p. 221.

8. *Ibid.*, p. 245.

9. The word *homily* means sermon. Hence the branch of seminary instruction that teaches preaching is called Homiletics.

10. *Calvin College Chimes*, May 6, 1966.

Chapter 15

1. This name is to be distinguished from Presbyterian Church in America, the name of a body that came into existence in the mid-seventies.

2. Quoted from *Harpers Magazine*, Jan. 1933, by Rian, *The Presbyterian Conflict*, pp. 138ff.

4. Quoted from *The Christian Century*, Nov. 23, 1932, by Stonehouse, *J. Gresham Machen*, p. 473.

4. Quoted by Stonehouse, *Ibid.*, pp. 486f. from *The Presbyterian*, July 19, 1936.

5. "Reflections on the Machen Trial," *The Banner*, May 3, 1935.

6. Stonehouse, *Ibid.*, p. 501.

7. *Ibid.*, pp. 501f.

8. R.B. Kuiper, "The Presbyterian Church of America," *The Banner*, July 3, 1936.

9. "Taking the Reformed Faith Seriously," *The Banner*, July 15, 1937.

10. Minutes of the Twelfth General Assembly 1945, p. 74.

11. *Ibid.*, p. 85.

12. Minutes of the Thirteenth General Assembly 1946, p. 91.

13. Minutes of the Twelfth General Assembly 1945.

14. Minutes of the Thirteenth General Assembly of the Orthodox Presbyterian Church, pp. 38-89, 112.

15. One wishing to gain further insight into this complex case can consult Fred H. Klooster's doctoral dissertation on "The Incomprehensibility of God in the Orthodox Presbyterian Conflict," Franeker, T. Wever, 1951. Another view of this case in its setting in the history of the Orthodox Presbyterian Church can be gained from a pamphlet by Edward Heerema entitled "Whither the Orthodox Presbyterian Church?" privately printed, 1947.

16. Citations from this report are taken from the type-written manuscript found among R.B.'s papers.

Chapter 16

1. *Acts of Synod 1952*, p. 95.

2. *Ibid.*, p. 97.

3. *Ibid.*, p. 116.

4. The four men dismissed from the faculty were appointed in 1943, 1944, 1948 and 1951.

5. From a manuscript found among R.B. Kuiper's papers. The author does not know when or where it was published.

Chapter 17

1. *The Banner*, Jan. 24, 1936.

Chapter 18

1. *To Be or Not To Be Reformed*, Zondervan Publishing House, Grand Rapids, Michigan, 1959, p. 192.

2. *Ibid.*, p. 194.

3. *Ibid.*, p. 147.

4. LeRoy B. Oliver, review in *The Westminster Theological Journal*, November 1960, pp. 68ff.

5. *God-Centered Evangelism*, Baker Book House, 1961, p. 84.

6. *Ibid.*, p. 159.

7. *Torch and Trumpet*, Vol. 1, No. 1, p. 1. April-May 1951.

8. "Is Dr. Boer Right?" *Torch and Trumpet*, Dec. 1957, pp. 11-14.

9. *Torch and Trumpet*, Nov. 1960, p. 14.

10. *Torch and Trumpet*, May-June, 1963, p. 8.

11. *Acts of Synod 1959*, pp. 571f.

12. *Torch and Trumpet*, May-June 1963, p. 10.

13. "Professor Harold Dekker on God's Universal Love," *Torch and Trumpet*, March 1963.

14. "Some Conclusions as to the Love of God," *Torch and Trumpet*, May-June, 1964.

15. *Torch and Trumpet*, May-June, 1963, p. 12. Quotation is from *The Reformed Journal*, Feb. 1963, where the article appeared.

16. *Ibid.*, p. 13.

17. *Acts of Synod 1959*, p. 46.

18. For R.B.'s views on the TCNN matter see *To Be or Not To Be Reformed*, pp. 177ff.

19. R.B.'s views on Antithesis are found in fullest detail in *The Encyclopedia of Christianity*, ed. Edwin H. Palmer, Vol. I, pp. 286ff. Henry Stob's views on the subject appear in *Perspectives on the Christian Reformed Church*, ed. De Klerk and De Ridder, Baker Book House, 1983, pp. 241-258.

20. The above account of this incident is gleaned from my memory of conversations with R.B. and from the record of it in *Torch and Trumpet*, July-August 1963, pp. 10f. Bearing on the incident was the decision of Synod 1961 to limit the advisory function of emeriti professors at synod to occasions when they would be asked for advice.

21. The address appeared in print in *The Banner* of June 16, 1961; and in *Torch and Trumpet*, April 1970.

22. The verbal contents of these sight-sound productions are available on cassette tapes from the Mt. Olive Tape Library, Inc., P.O. Box 422, Mt. Olive, MS 39119.

23. *The Presbyterian Guardian*, May 1963, p. 67.

24. R.B. Kuiper, *The Bible Tells Us So*, The Banner of Truth Trust, London, 1968, p. 15.

Chapter 19

1. From personal letter to the author dated Jan. 21, 1984.

2. *To Be or Not To Be Reformed*, pp. 144f.

3. Carl Eugene Zylstra, *God-Centered Preaching in a Human-Centered Age*—The Developing Crisis Confronting a Conservative Calvinist Theology of Preaching in the Christian Reformed Church 1935-1975. A Dissertation Submitted to the Faculty of Princeton Theological Seminary in Partial Fulfillment of the Requirement for the Degree of Doctor of Philosophy. Princeton, New Jersey, 1983. Quotations from pages 165-174.

4. *The Bible Tells Us So*, p. 8.

5. John Bolt, *Christian and Reformed Today*, Paideia Press, Jordan Station, Ontario, 1984, pp. 23f.

6. *To Be or Not To Be Reformed*, p. 126.

7. *Torch and Trumpet*, March 1961, p. 3. See also "The Balance that is Calvinism," *The Calvin Forum*, August-September 1952, pp. 9ff

8 *Religion and Culture*, April 1922, pp. 161ff. I have positive evidence that the unsigned editorial was written by R.B. Kuiper.

9. R.B. Kuiper, *The Glorious Body of Christ*, Eerdmans, Grand Rapids, 1958, p. 12.

10. "The Church and Ecumenism," in *To Be or Not To Be Reformed*, pp. 176f.